25
MOUNTAIN BIKE TOURS
in New Jersey

25 MOUNTAIN BIKE TOURS
in New Jersey

Peter Kick

Backcountry Publications

Woodstock · Vermont

An invitation to the reader

The trails, signs, and landmarks along these tours—and especially the regulations governing them—are highly subject to change over time. Please check with each park's management for current conditions. And if you find that such changes have occurred on these routes, please let the author and publisher know, so that corrections may be made in future editions. Other comments and suggestions are also welcome. Address all correspondence to:

Editor, 25 Bicycle Tours Series
Backcountry Publications
PO Box 748, Woodstock, Vermont 05091

Library of Congress Cataloging-in-Publication Data

Kick, Peter
25 mountain bike tours in New Jersey / Peter Kick.
        p.   cm.
Includes bibliographical references (p.   ).
ISBN 0-88150-386-X (alk. paper)
1. All terrain cycling—New Jersey—Guidebooks. 2. New Jersey—Guidebooks. I. Title.
GV1045.5.N5K53 1997
796.6'3'09749—dc21   97-12812
                                    CIP

Text design by Sally Sherman
Cover design by Susan Wheeler
Cover photograph by Brian Bailey/Tony Stone Images
Interior photos by the author
Maps by Dick Widhu, © 1997 The Countryman Press

Published by Backcountry Publications,
a division of The Countryman Press
PO Box 748, Woodstock, VT 05091

Distributed by W. W. Norton & Company, Inc.
500 Fifth Avenue, New York, NY 10110

Printed in the United States of America
10 9 8 7 6 5 4 3

Acknowledgments

I'd like to recognize a number of people for their contribution to this effort—and to the future of mountain biking in New Jersey: Wally Tunison, IMBA representative for the state of New Jersey and founder/president of the New Jersey Cycling Conservation Club; Lyle Lange, IMBA representative for Northwestern New Jersey, and founder of KIMBA; Bob Holderith, IMBA representative in Northeast New Jersey; Marty Epstein, owner, Mark Traeger, philosopher, Steve Owens, evil minion, and David Dziemian, super mechanic, of Marty's Reliable Cycle, birthplace of JORBA (Jersey Off-Road Bicycling Association) and Sarah Frost, NORBA Rep, founder of JORBA and the Paydirt Program (Paydirt gives race points in exchange for time spent doing trail maintenance); Ken Thoman, trails planner and ecologist, and Mack Ford, park ranger, Monmouth County Parks Commission; Christian Bethmann, superintendent, and Pat Perry, parks assistant, Lebanon State Forest; Tom Hoffman, park historian, Gateway National Recreation Area, Sandy Hook Unit; Barbara Leon, state park ranger, and Colleen Ruzika, park manager, and their geese at Bull's Island Recreation Area; Greg Ardire, forest ranger, Parvin State Park; Carol Forbes, assistant superintendent, High Point State Park; Bart Wallin, superintendent, and George Sloff, park ranger, Allamuchy Mountain State Park; Pam Thier, planner, Hunterdon County Park Commission; Al Schweikert, mayor of High Bridge, and his staff; Brian Schmult, chairman, New Jersey Rail Trails; Len Frank, president, Paulinskill Valley Trail Committee; John Auciello, chief ranger, Delaware and Raritan Canal State Park; Joyce Shaffer, Orange Key Guide service coordinator, Princeton University; Susan Barbarisi of The Open Space Institute; Karen Votava, chairperson, East Coast Greenway Alliance; T. Mark Pitchell, superintendent, and Chief Ranger Lou Casper, Ringwood State Park; Fritz Jenkins, facilities maintenance chief, Pequannock Watershed; Bob Goodman, superintendent, Wawayanda State Park; Mark Bettinger, regional representative, Sierra Club; Barry Sullivan, New Jersey district ranger, and Frank Valentine, ranger, Delaware Water Gap National Recreation Area; Daniel Chazin, NYNJTC Publications Committee; Patricia Strickland, research; Bob Moss, NYNJTC Ringwood supervisor and Highlands Trail chairman; Dale Williams, sales representative, The Bicycle Hub at Cheesequake; the folks at Rambo's in Califon, especially the chef; Don Potter, biker, from the Pizza House Restaurant in Milford, PA; and all the others whose names I didn't get or lost, including the anonymous riders encountered on the trails. Thanks also to mountain bikers Tim Mikesh, student, of Rockaway, and John Salamone, New Jersey state trooper, of Boonton, for guiding services at Tourne Park.

Thanks especially to my support people and test riders: June Sanson-Kick, my wife, Ryan Peter Kick, my son, and his crew, Tim Gifford, Grace Gifford, and William (BJ) and Lauren Dellolio; to Hugh Christie, riding companion, and Susan Christie, rider and typist; and to Al White, my local wing man, mud-shunner, and exercise partner.

I am gratefully, irrevocably indebted to this book's spiritual guardian and editor, Laura Jorstad, whom I'm sure would rather have been fly-fishing or at least editing fly-fishing books; to Dale Gelfand; and to Helen Whybrow, editor in chief, Cristen Brooks, production editor, and the staff at Backcountry Publications for their dedication, expertise, and commitment to excellence.

For Ryan Peter Kick

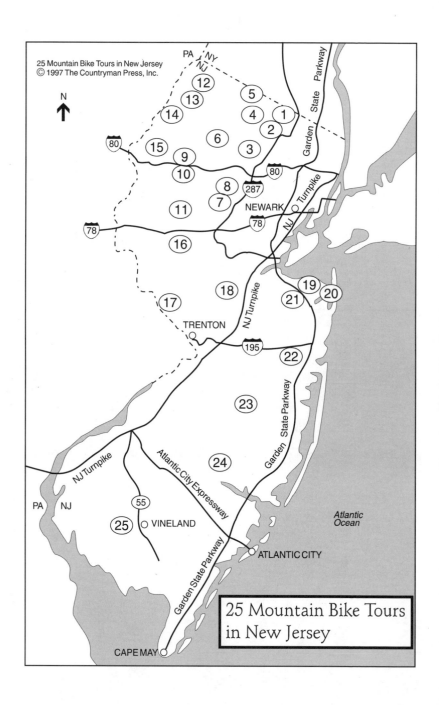

25 Mountain Bike Tours in New Jersey
© 1997 The Countryman Press, Inc.

N

PA
NY
NJ

Garden State Parkway

80

80

287

NEWARK

NJ Turnpike

78

78

NJ Turnpike

195

Garden State Parkway

NJ Turnpike

PA

NJ

55

VINELAND

Atlantic City Expressway

Garden State Parkway

Atlantic
Ocean

ATLANTIC CITY

TRENTON

CAPE MAY

25 Mountain Bike Tours
in New Jersey

Contents

HIGHLANDS PROVINCE   29

RIDGE AND VALLEY PROVINCE   95

PIEDMONT PROVINCE   125

Author's Note

It is my wish that this book will serve as a positive influence toward the development and appreciation of mountain biking in the state of New Jersey. I want it to be a resource for trail users as well as trail planners; to provide a record of mountain biking in the state as it currently exists, thus helping to serve the sport's future writers, practitioners, and advocates; and to aid in the creation of sensible user patterns in those parks where they don't already exist. I want this book to be a step in the right direction—to promote cooperation among agencies, organizations, and trail users; to be part of the solutions instead of the problems facing trail designation in New Jersey's pressured parklands. And the problems are real.

Like most of you, I use trails for many purposes. (In the current parlance, I'm a *multiple user.*) The outdoor pursuits we enjoy range from hiking to biking, from Nordic skiing to in-line skating, from climbing to snowboarding and whatever else it is we need space for. I think it's fair to say that we are all interested in and connected to the wildlands we use—that we care about them and are concerned about their condition. Some of us are wilderness-first types, who use our chosen methods of recreation simply to experience nature. Others of us are fitness-first types, more preoccupied with the means of travel than with the environment traveled through.

But what both groups must remember is that the environment is always important. We benefit from wilderness whether we know it or not and even whether we want to or not. We benefit psychologically from wilderness even if we don't use it—just from knowing it's there, from realizing that we can use it if we want to, that even if we don't understand just how, it's important to our health and to our lives and to our children's lives.

If I ever have to choose between preservation of the wilderness and preservation of my sport, I'll drop the sport in a minute (then look for someplace else to ride) and contribute to the health or the design or the

maintenance of the land until it can take the impact of my bike. That is the guiding philosophy behind this book.

Still, problems have arisen, because we multiple users are new on the scene. Hikers were here before us, and for decades—even generations—they have advocated and fought for open space acquisition, planned and maintained the trails, and paid and repaid their dues maybe more than any other generation will ever have to (that remains to be seen). They think of multiple use, if they think of it at all (not having had to much until now) as hiking and Nordic skiing—which, of course, it is. But this definition is expanding radically—exponentially—at a very fast pace.

Mechanized sports have created a deep rift between the traditional user group—hikers—and those of us lately arrived on the scene. These traditional recreationists have seen the mountain bikers—the flashy new user group, the mechanized user group—on the very trails they helped to acquire or build, prompting thoughts like, "Wait . . . is this right? Has what I've done been in vain?" They see accelerated erosion. They perceive brash attitudes. They watch parks reel from the sudden impact. They see anything but what they want to see. And they see it mechanized. They see the final, figurative end of Eden. Here it is, after years of nothing but footprints and photographs: The machine is in the garden.

But again, the garden—the wilderness—is of benefit to all of us. It's the greatest single human resource. That's the solution, according to present thought: Trails designed and designated for a variety of users. And if we bikers, equestrians, wheelchair users, skiers, and mountain boarders don't want one user group dictating what trails we're going to use, now is the time to get involved.

I see an incredible number of young people on mountain bikes. Sometimes I want to tell traditional recreationists, who see this force as a threat instead of an advantage, to wait. Listen. No matter how they're dressed or how they act or what they ride—or what part of their body is pierced—this is the group that will inherit what's left of the earth. And I don't have to tell you what kind of a job that's going to be. Aren't you glad they're not meek?

> *We can all get together on this thing in the interest of the resource, or we can stand divided and see the resouce compromised.*
>
> Wally Tunison, New Jersey IMBA representative

Your actions on your next ride will influence which trails will be open for bicycle use in the years to come.

The North Jersey Mountain Bike Club

I assure you that we recognize the popularity of mountain bicycles and do not intend to exclude their use from park lands.

T. Mark Pitchell, superintendent, Ringwood State Park

Whereas mountain bikers are a legitimate user group sharing the county park trails with hikers, equestrians and other park patrons . . . these guidelines shall be designed to protect the interest of all park patrons who wish to use the trail systems . . . within these valuable resources.

Morris County Park Commission By-Laws

Introduction

As a New Yorker, venturing into New Jersey to ride and research mountain bike trails has given me a new perspective on the sport and reaffirmed just how seriously it's regarded by its enthusiasts. New Jersey has the most involved and progressive cycling community I've ever seen. Witness the number of bike clubs and organizations you can find here, the number of cycling publications, road touring guides, cycling paths, multiuse trails, bike-legal park roadways, and state and county parks that advertise mountain biking trails. Not to mention the highly organized and active rail-trails group (NJRT) and the many advocacy organizations that solidly back, promote, and lobby the sport (these organizations are listed in the appendix).

Pick up a copy of Jersey's *Cycling Times* and browse the cycling calendar, local club board, and race reports; you'll see how organized New Jersey's cyclists are. You'll also find advocacy information, New York club listings and ride schedules, fun and charity rides information, and an extensive ride-partners section. *Cycling Times* calls itself "the Northeast's Most Complete Cycling Calendar," and I think that's correct. For riders new to the area, *Cycling Times* is required reading (available free at most bike shops or by subscription). It will help you zero in on your area of interest and simplify your search for the shops and clubs that ride there. Shop and club riders encourage nonmembers, and many off-road rides are open to all ability levels.

So what's going on? Why New Jersey's popularity among cyclists? One reason may simply be its population density—more people per square mile than any other state. Its parks and forests are pressured by dense populations of mountain bikers, who have accordingly organized to support their wildlands in increasing numbers.

The NJDOT

Another reason for cycling's popularity in New Jersey is the state's Department of Transportation. The NJDOT recognizes the bicycle's importance to the state's welfare, noting both its environmental and personal benefits:

- It doesn't degrade the environment
- It requires no nonrenewable energy resources
- It's inexpensive to own and operate
- It promotes fitness and a sense of well-being (and it's fun)

The NJDOT states that its policy is to "promote the increased use of the bicycle . . . to address and accommodate the needs [of bicycle traffic] . . . in the development of state-funded transportation projects and programs." It also encourages and consults to other state, regional, county, and local agencies to "adopt policies and implement programs [that] will enhance the cycling environment."

Specifically, but not exclusively, these policies apply to the roadways of New Jersey—and as such they apply more to the touring cyclist than the off-road rider. However, there's considerable overlap between the two groups. (Just look at the hybrid bicycle and at the promotion and legislation of road travel as well as trail use.) One serves the other. If cycling lanes and bike paths are included in future road planning, bicycle use will inevitably increase. (And if the world made sense, as pollution and congestion of our highways increased, there would be tax incentives for buying and using bicycles—such as no sales tax on new bikes—and for decreasing your annual gasoline consumption.) Even as things are in the United States, more bicycles are sold than automobiles, and most bikes are purchased by adults.

Aside from sleek recumbents, many cycles of the future will be commuter-driven, street-fighting ATBs, like the hybrids and mountain bikes of today. And the same people who commute on their mountain bikes will be using them for recreation during their leisure time. I believe the ATB will evolve into the ideal, all-purpose, alternative means of transport (along with your solar electric automobile). The already huge and growing group of cyclists will be looking for, promoting, and developing dedicated bike paths and off-road riding opportunities, as well as electing—or acting as—the officials who will support their interests. I believe the current promotion of commuter cycling will lead inevitably to greater interest and participation in all aspects of the sport and will inevitably stimulate the proactive side of the cycling community. Soon enough, every municipality, township, and state and county park will be linked by bikeways (take a look at what Morris County has

Along the Paulinskill Valley Trail

done already) and will have no choice but to develop management policies for cyclists, both on and off-road, where they don't already exist and where the need for them is obvious and appropriate.

The NJDOT is currently working on a dozen bike path projects throughout the state. The most interesting one at this point—at least to New York–area cyclists—is the $11.2 million path that will run from the New Jersey side of the George Washington Bridge north to the New York State border. This will be an alternative route to US 9W, a road that has been used by hordes of serious touring cyclists for years as the only suitable egress from greater New York. It will be constructed on the green-strip between US 9W and the Palisades Interstate Parkway. Other projects include the Rocky Brook Parkway, Camden County Ped/ Bike Extensions, Somerset Transit Access, Atlantic Highlands Section of the Bayshore Trail, George Street Bikeway, Trenton Bikeway, and a route from Stirling to Millington.

The NJNYTC

Substantial credit is also owed to hikers for the creation of regional trail systems, many of which are used by cyclists. New Jersey hikers enjoy a long history of trail building and maintenance by merit of the New York–New Jersey Trail Conference, a nearly century-old organization that does a great deal more for the conservation of open space in the state than most other nonprofit organizations have. In terms of preserving natural resources and advocating funds for or themselves funding—the acquisition of public lands, we all owe this group and its hundreds of smaller constituent organizations a tremendous debt.

NORBA, IMBA, JORBA, KIMBA, and the NJCCC

Do these names sound like Nordic gods and goddesses? If so, that would be appropriate, because I can't help feeling that this book has been a classical odyssey, a struggle of order over chaos and faith over disillusion, complete with its Sirens and Cyclops.

    Considerable obstacles face the growth and accommodation of mountain biking in this state (and many others). I've seen infighting among park managers over the issue of trail designation and upkeep. I've listened as parks people lamented the broken promises of volunteer groups who offered to assist and never came forward. I've seen rangers ticketing and locking the gate on overzealous late bikers, asking me sincerely as they wrote the tickets, "Do they think I've nothing to do but wait for them?" I've heard rangers swear to me that they will close the trails, telling me, "This situation won't last." I've been told that the appearance of a mountain bike book for New Jersey was premature. I've spoken with errant bikers who said that they'd been threatened and thrown off multiple-use trails by the people responsible for their upkeep.

But I've seen the bright side, too. I meet a growing number of park managers who are excited about the prospect of mountain bikers visiting their trails. I see clubs building these same trails. I've seen park managers on mountain bikes. I've been handed *bike* trail maps as I've entered state parks and forests. I see a growing number of trails designed and designated for off-road bikes. I'm told by members of the biking and hiking communities that a trail guidebook is sorely needed to help establish separate user patterns and to stimulate thoughts about approaching our wildlands as forces joined instead of divided. I meet club riders and shop owners who are adopting trails and parks, working closely with management, scheduling work days, maintaining trails. And let's not overlook the economic shot in the arm that we all see going into our understaffed, underfunded local parks in the form of admission fees.

I see everybody from renegade kids who need to be reeled in a little to contented athletes and sport riders—who are doing some of that reeling—to middle-aged couples to grinning families who've found an activity they can participate in together that's more fun even than . . . hiking. I pull into county parks and read signboards that say WELCOME, MOUNTAIN BIKERS.

My quest has been aided by these organizations with their endearing acronyms: the National Off-Road Bicycle Association, International Mountain Bike Association, Jersey Off-Road Bicycle Association, Kittatiny Mountain Biking Association, and the New Jersey Cycling Conservation Club (endearing even without an acronym). The future of off-road riding in the state depends heavily on their presence, guardianship, and dedication.

Now that I've biked around New Jersey for a year and a half, I see the ways to repay the forces of good. How is this done? By getting involved with your local trail-access group. By joining or forming a club dedicated to trail access and maintenence. By patronizing—or owning—a bike shop that provides advocacy as well as bicycles.

Sugar Sand: Allaire State Park

Notes for Using This Guide

New Jersey Trails

In my quest for viable mountain bike trails in New Jersey's state parks, forests, and recreation areas, I've found that, as a rule, you can't rely on finding good rides (if any) in most facilities under 1000 acres in size. There are exceptions to this, of course, such as the 727-acre Stephens State Park, which is managed effectively for multiple use, and the many county parks, where size is secondary to accessibility (sometimes a 3-mile ride close to home is better than a 10-mile ride farther away). If all the trails in a 1000-acre park are open to bikes, you can get about an 8-mile ride without too much repetition. In larger forests, such as Wharton (110,000 acres), there are literally hundreds of miles of trails and roads. The typical size of a New Jersey state park that promotes mountain biking and can direct the impact of such promotion weighs in at around 3000 to 10,000 acres, and these are the meccas where 10- or 20-mile (legal) loops are not uncommon. Obviously, management is the key. Even a tiny county park can handle impact if it's managed intelligently. And remember: A park's carrying capacity increases in correlation to effective management and the education of its users.

Mileage

The mile marks in this book (for reasons discussed under "Cyclo-computers and Cyclometers") must be considered guidelines, not absolutes. They're given in hundredths of a mile in some cases. Don't expect your cyclometer to reflect the book's mile measurements for any given tour. It won't. While the intent is to give an accurate, overall tour distance, individual readings for specified turns and landmarks will vary from your own. Accordingly, use the given mileage as a reference, and where it is suggested in the text, carry the appropriate maps and refer to them, as well as to landmarks, for direction finding.

Cyclocomputers and Cyclometers

Cyclocomputers are among the more fidgety and accident-prone gadgets on the bicycling accessory list. Most mountain bikes on the trails today aren't equipped with them. Off-road riders are not as concerned with mileage as touring bikers, and all the wiring and wheel- and spoke-mounted hardware is a liability in the brushy, bumpy, brash environment of the off-road cycle. In general, the more expensive and complicated these gadgets become, the less reliable they are on mountain bikes. Even wireless models still have a larger fork-mounted sensor-transmitter than wired models. This much fragile mass low down on your fork is undesirable. Also, proximity to whirring machinery (like your car's motor) may drive them wild. Wireless models are also known to interfere with heart rate monitors and are susceptible to microwave transmission (cellular phones). Thus, new "interference-free" models have appeared on the market.

Speed and distance readings are nice to have, but some of the other cycle computer features are gimmicky and redundant. Maximum and average speed, clock and stopwatch (what about your wristwatch?), dual-interval timers, training summaries, programmable multiple bicycle calibration, calorie counters, and built-in heart rate limit warnings (what next?) are all useful training tools but quickly add to the complexity and distraction of the ride.

Even a reliable cyclometer is prone to inaccuracies. Differences in calibration when mounting (figuring the correct wheel circumference), surface wheel spin, car-rack wheel spin (take your cycle computer off while traveling), carrying your bike, and that particular human error, forgetting to reset the device, will all influence your readings. If you get one, ask your dealer for the simplest, most reliable model—which is usually the cheapest—and let the dealer install it. Then, compare your trip distances with friends (and maps) to see if you're accurate. If you're not acceptably accurate with a map or measured mile, you'll need to recalibrate.

Safety and Precautions

Many of these tours take you close to dangerous drops, steep trailside ravines, and some overhead rock. Precipitous and potentially hazardous terrain is home to the mountain bike, but your discretion must be exercised to ensure a happy and safe experience. Be especially alert when traveling with children. Be firm and repetitive with them and insist on helmets. Ride ahead of them when potential hazards are discussed in the text. Walk when you're near dangerous cliffs.

Carry a small first-aid kit with several large Band-Aids, a gauze pad, and some antiseptic. Leave these at the bottom of your handlebar bag or underseat bag. You may not need to apply a Band-Aid to a small cut or abrasion, but kids really like them, and giving them the extra attention will help to maintain morale.

Carry extra food, water, and clothing. If you get lost, have a breakdown, or find yourself delayed for any reason, these items will help. Remember—bicyclists are susceptible to exposure, too.

Tools and Flats

Going afield without tools is risky. You may be in for a long walk for want of just an Allen wrench. People walking their bikes in a state of dejection will often ask if you have a certain tool. An excellent if not mandatory investment—which you can shove into your wedge, bar, or frame pack and forget about—is one of the multitools offered by bicycle pro shops and mail-order companies. Some are better than others— you'll discover this someday while trying to extract and replace a chain rivet with an inferior chain tool while sweat drips from your body and mosquitoes assault your back. Buy a good one. They contain (almost) everything you'll ever need "and nothing you don't" for minor trail repairs.

What they won't do, however, is fix flats. You've got to carry at least two tire levers and a patch kit if your tool set doesn't include them (some do). You can carry an extra tube if you want, but still bring the patch kit. Spare tubes are cheap. You're also going to need a pump or source to air up after a flat. If you know you've got a puncture, you can always add a little "slime" as you reinflate, which seals punctures up to about 3/16 inch in diameter. Then inflate with either your pump or CO_2 inflation device. The latter fit any valve, and some handle any size cartridge. Don't expect to achieve perfection on your first try with an inflator, however. It takes a little practice. Until you're good at it, carry extra CO_2 cartridges. The only advantage inflators have over pumps is the speed of the fill. Otherwise, they lean toward the gimmicky. (Note: Local trail advocacy is better supported by purchasing your cycling needs from local shops. Mail-order companies have contributed nothing to New Jersey trails.)

Lighting Systems

I don't use or recommend fixed lighting on a mountain bike unless your primary use will be street riding. In that case, investing in a good system (and some can be quite the investment—over $200) may be worth it. For rides in the backcountry that last until dark—and sometimes they do whether we planned it that way or not—it's best to carry a strap-on headlamp. These are very reliable and reasonably priced these days, and their main advantage is that they look where you look—something you'll really come to appreciate if you ride uneven terrain at night. Another good thing to have is a taillight, like the kind that blink continuously and mount on a simple seat-post adaptor. With the combination of the headlamp and taillight, you'll be in good shape for back-road traffic. Be sure your taillight is not obscured by your wedge pack, jacket, or rack baggage. Leave the reflectors that came with your new bike where they are. Look for other lightweight and reliable lights that you can carry easily.

Sound Systems

New Jersey transportation law requires you to have a horn or bell mounted on your handlebars. Pass pedestrians slowly after "ringing" them well in advance. In my experience, horns tend to startle, while bells will actually make people smile. Try it and see.

Riding Technique

Read up on climbing and descending if you haven't done so yet. Learn which brake lever operates which brake. Learn about out-of-saddle positions, pedal positions, brake feathering, and things like "letting go"—gaining enough speed to clear obstacles that would send you over the bars at lower speeds (there are books available on the subject; check out this book's appendix).

About Maps

If the map provided with the tour you're taking isn't detailed enough for you and you want to explore further, I've suggested additional maps, if and where appropriate, in each tour heading. Most of the parks and facilities you'll visit will have an official or "bootleg" map handout, and the maps in this book are generally based on them. But maps are not always available or useful for trail navigation or even as base maps sometimes. In those cases, try using US Geographical Survey (USGS) topographic quadrangles. While many of the regular topo sheets you can buy at sporting goods stores aren't updated frequently enough to reflect trail changes, and they don't always show trails or small double-tracks, they are good for noting historic and established routes—which can also help you orient yourself. They're also considered the best maps for land navigation purposes and represent the only comprehensive mapping coverage of the state.

You'll find that county maps and regional atlases and gazetteers are the most useful aids for getting you to and from tour sites. Normally these don't contain enough detail or topographic information to be used in the type of land navigation an all-terrain cyclist might find necessary. So if you do plan to leave the trails suggested in the tours, be reasonably sure that, first, you're not venturing onto private property (which should be posted), and second, you have the appropriate USGS map for the area. Order these from the addresses following, or try to buy them near the tour location. They're often sold in sporting goods stores, or are available at the local library for reference. If you expect to wander onto lands in proximity to large tracts of forest preserve—where it's possible to get lost for a long time—carry a compass and the additional supplies you'll need in the event of emergency.

The best maps for the parks and trails most commonly used by recreationists are the New York–New Jersey Trail Conference maps, which cover most of the northern New Jersey parks and some of the other trails or roads discussed in this book. Conference maps are an indispensable aid to any backcountry user. They contain all sorts of useful information regarding emergencies, bus timetables, clubs, weather, parks, phone numbers, and history. They are widely distributed and are easier to get hold of, on short notice, than USGS maps. To be sure, order your maps in advance or inquire at your local sporting goods and camping supplies store. More recently bike shops have begun carrying them and will often prove to be a great source of odd maps, pirated overlays, and standard topographic maps. Ask around.

To order maps:

New York–New Jersey Trail Conference (NYNJTC)
GPO Box 2250
New York, NY 10116
212-685-9699
www.nynjtc.org/

US Geological Survey
Branch of Information Services
Box 25286, Denver Federal Center
Denver, CO 80225
303-202-4700

Biker's Checklist

Day Trips
full water bottle or backpack hydration system
cycling shorts
helmet
sunglasses
gloves
first-aid kit

lock
tire repair tools and patches
pump or CO_2 inflator
extra tube
basic tool kit
maps
food bars or gel packets
lunch/snack
sunscreen
insect repellent
rain gear

Optional but Useful Items (Especially for Longer Tours)
panniers (saddlebags)
handlebar bag
rack strap
headlamp and taillight
batteries
journal
camera
towel/swimsuit
windbreaker

International Mountain Biking Association Rules of the Trail

1. **Ride on open trails only.** Respect trail and road closures (ask if not sure), avoid possible trespass on private land, obtain permits and authorization as may be required. Federal and State wilderness areas are closed to cycling.
2. **Leave no trace.** Be sensitive to the dirt beneath you. Even on open trails, you should not ride under conditions where you will leave evidence of your passing, such as on certain soils shortly after a rain. Observe the different types of soils and trail construction; practice low-impact cycling. This also means staying on the trail and not creating any new ones. Pack out at least as much as you pack in.
3. **Control your bicycle.** Inattention for even a second can cause problems. Obey all speed laws.
4. **Always yield the trail.** Make known your approach well in advance. A friendly greeting (or a bell) is considerate and works well; don't startle others. Show your respect when passing others by slowing to a walk or even stopping. Anticipate that other trail users may be around corners or in blind spots.
5. **Never spook animals.** All animals are startled by an unannounced approach, a sudden movement, or a loud noise. This can be dangerous for you, for others, and for the animals. Give animals extra room and time to adjust to you. In passing, use special care and follow the directions of horseback riders (ask if uncertain). Running cattle and disturbing wild animals are serious offenses. Leave gates as you found them, or as marked.
6. **Plan ahead.** Know your equipment, your ability, and the area in which you are riding—and prepare accordingly. Be self-sufficient at all times. Wear a helmet, keep your machine in good condition, and carry necessary supplies for changes in weather or other conditions. A well-executed trip is a satisfaction to you and not a burden or offense to others.

—Reprinted by permission of the International
Mountain Biking Association (IMBA)

HIGHLANDS PROVINCE

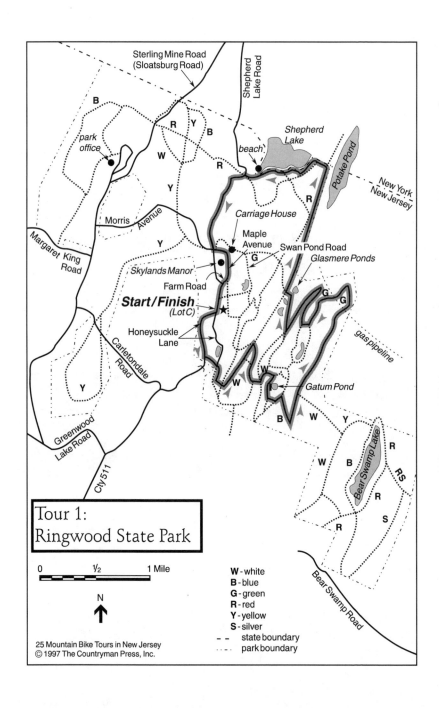

Sterling Mine Road
(Sloatsburg Road)

Shepherd Lake Road

B

park
office

R **Y** **B**

W

Shepherd
Lake

beach

Potake Pond

New York
New Jersey

R

Y

R

Morris Avenue

Carriage House

Y

Maple
Avenue

Swan Pond Road
Glasmere Ponds

Margaret King Road

Skylands Manor

G

Farm Road

Start/Finish
(Lot C)

G **G**

Honeysuckle
Lane

gas pipeline

Carletondale Road

Y

W

W

Gatum Pond

B **W**

Y

Greenwood Lake Road

W **B**

Bear Swamp Lake

R

Cty 511

RS

R

Tour 1:
Ringwood State Park

S

R

0   ½   1 Mile

W - white
B - blue
G - green
R - red
Y - yellow
S - silver
- - state boundary
... park boundary

N

Bear Swamp Road

25 Mountain Bike Tours in New Jersey
© 1997 The Countryman Press, Inc.

1

Ringwood State Park

Location: *Ringwood Township, Passaic County*
Distance: *10.35-mile loop; many other legal trails exist*
Terrain: *Hilly*
Surface: *Variable; carriage roads with steep, rocky sections and single-track*
Maps: *Ringwood State Park, State Park Service (free); NYNJTC, North Jersey Trails, Trail Map #22 (recommended)*
Highlights: *State Botanical Garden; miles of cycling terrain with single-track trails currently being identified and and designated; Shepherd Lake; swimming, boating, fishing, romantic strolling, and picnicking*

Ask almost any mountain biker in North Jersey about good places to ride, and you'll hear the name Ringwood—either from experience or a desire to go check out the word of mouth about its great singletrack trails. Also, park management and policies are very progressive and biker-friendly; an established, proactive group of club cyclists—namely the Ramapo Valley Cycling Club—has become involved in trail advocacy, management, and maintenance; and NORBA-sanctioned events take place there on an established singletrack course. With the onset of the off-road biking community over the past decade, the park has endured the usual growing pains, and some debate has surrounded bike use and trail designation. North Jersey riders have been happy to see that state park management, despite staffing difficulties, has proven effective.

Long a favorite of metropolitan hikers and the NYNJTC, Ringwood's use quotas are high, and so is sentiment. Undoubtedly, some areas of the park have seen increasing impact by bikers (and hikers). Its user patterns have only recently come under the scrutiny and direction of the

New Jersey Trails Plan (approved in 1982), which should finally lead to the official designation of Ringwood trails. Park managers will grin as they tell you that the plan was due to be in place by June 1994—but it does look as if it'll be in place by the summer of 1997. They hope.

The plan will identify more legal singletrack in the park. Parks people are more than willing to promote mountain biking at Ringwood— they get nearly a hundred times as many inquiries from bikers as from hikers. More biking means, in general, more public participation and service; in particular, more dollars for strapped park budgets. Once you get to Ringwood and see all the other mountain bikers, you'll think you're someplace special. Once you ride the park a little, you'll know you are.

From the New York side of the border, Ringwood Park can be reached from the Sloatsburg area via the New York State Thruway, NY 17, or NY 59. In New Jersey, it's accessible from the west via County Route (CR) 91 (Skyline Drive going north from Oakland) and Sloatsburg Road.

From exit 15A on the NYS Thruway, go north on NY 17 (this is also NY 59 at this point) to a sign on the right reading RINGWOOD STATE PARK (2 miles if you were southbound on the NYS Thruway and got off at 15A or 1.4 miles if you were northbound). Turn right at the sign. This is Sterling Mine Road (sometimes known as Sloatsburg Road). The park is 5 miles ahead. You're going to the Skylands section; to reach it, drive 0.4 mile past the Ringwood State Park entrance and turn left onto Morris Avenue, toward Shepherd Lake.

At 2 miles you'll reach the entrance booth. There's a small parking fee. Going to Shepherd Lake will cost you a few dollars more, which isn't necessary, since you can bike there for free. If you don't plan to use the beach, park in lot C, where the mountain bikers park. You'll most likely be directed to that lot. (You can still ride your bike the short distance to Shepherd Lake and use the lake for no charge.)

To reach parking lot C, pay the entrance fee, get your (free) Ringwood State Park map, and turn right. Leaving the Carriage House to your left (there are phones and rest rooms here), pass Skylands Manor on your right as you proceed along Maple Avenue. At 0.2 mile bear right onto Farm Road, then bear left, passing parking lot B on your right. At the next intersection, bear left into parking lot C.

The park's history began in 1740 when the iron forges and furnaces of the Ringwood Company supplied the colonies through the American Revolution to the late 19th century. One of the largest attractions at Ringwood is the New Jersey State Botanical Garden at Skylands. It's the only botanical garden in the state park system and worth a visit. Flowers are in bloom throughout the season. From parking lot C you can easily tour the botanical gardens in a large loop of just under 2 miles by following Swan Pond Road from the upper right-hand corner (northeast) of the lot. Bearing left on the white trail will take you past the Four Continents Statues on Crab Apple Vista, past Swan Pond, the Wildflower and Bog Gardens, and past the inner park back to East Cottage Road and the Carriage House.

This tour will take you on the park's best doubletrack trails—ridable for bikers at most ability levels and worthwhile for everyone. It will also take you past the park's best singletrack trails, many of which will be open to bikers with the completion of the trails plan (which should be by the time you read this). You can also ride the racecourse, which you'll pass several times. It's currently a combination of double- and single-track trails, but this is subject to change.

Wherever you ride, carry a map. You can get lost in this park. Carry extra provisions, including first aid, water, and food. Use your head and your map. Marking is currently poor, the park map is impossible to navigate by accurately, and the NYNJTC map, although the best available, can be just as confusing. After riding the loop, however, you'll have a pretty good idea of the basic layout of the park. To begin, get on your bike and head back out of parking lot C.

0.00 *At the intersection of lot C and two paved roads, go diagonally across the intersection, bearing left onto Honeysuckle Lane (don't go hard left, against one-way traffic, or hard right, the way you came in). Follow the paved road, going slightly downhill. There's a low timber guardrail on your right. Pass the Skylands exit and a house on your right.*

0.70 *Just as paved Honeysuckle Lane turns 180 degrees, take the right-hand turn onto a dirt road with a barrier gate. A sign reads* MODEL PLANE FIELD. *The dirt road splits within 100 feet. Take the left fork and climb easily.*

1.26 *Pass a dirt road on your right.*

1.40 At a four-way intersection turn right on the (white) Crossover Trail. Marking here is fair. Watch carefully for white paint. Continue straight.

1.80 Arrive at an elongated Y and bear left. Immediately beyond is a hard left; don't take it. Continue straight. Follow white markers (which are sparse).

1.84 Arrive at a four-way intersection. Go straight onto a rocky road. You'll momentarily see white markers. The surface improves. Watch carefully for the white trail on your right.

2.00 Turn right to continue on the white trail, here a steep single-track. Arrive at Gatum Pond and go right, keeping the pond to your left. You're on an earthen dam at the northwest edge of the pond at this point. Climb easily.

2.22 Pass a small doubletrack on your right.

2.23 Pass another, wider road on your right.

2.27 You'll see the model plane field on your right. Keep going straight, passing a road on your left.

2.32 Arrive at a four-way intersection. Go through it, bearing left, following white blazes.

2.39 At a Y, the white trail switches back hard, uphill, to your right. Follow it and climb. Continue uphill through a hardwood forest. The trail switches back left before leveling out on Pierson Ridge.

3.28 Pass a trail on your right. At this unmarked intersection, the white trail heads southeast into the Bear Swamp area. Don't follow it. Keep going straight. Now you're on the blue Pierson Ridge trail.

3.33 Pass two or three more trails on your right within a few hundred feet of each other.

You'll see a small group of boulders on your left as the forest changes to white pine on your left, hardwoods on your right.

The road begins a gentle descent. Now you'll see some blue markers.

3.85 *At a four-way intersection, go straight across the gas pipeline.*

3.93 *At a Y, continue straight. The blue trail officially ends here, where you see three blue-paint markers on a tree as a right-hand road descends out of the park. Proceed straight ahead on the level carriageway. You're now officially on the green Halifax Trail.*

There are views to your right when the foliage is sparse.

Curve around through the North Cape, and you begin heading south again.

4.40 *Cross back over the pipeline at a four-way intersection, continuing straight ahead and descending.*

4.76 *Go right at a T.*

4.84 *At a Y—within sight of the previous T (4.76)—go right, downhill.*

5.23 *At a Y, the trail you're following (green) switches back and goes downhill. Keep left, following on green. There are paint blazes here.*

5.79 *Arrive at an elongated four-way intersection. Bear hard right, continuing downhill.*

6.10 *Pass a road on the left.*

6.20 *Pass between the Glasmere Ponds.*

6.23 *At a T, turn right onto a dirt doubletrack.*

6.40 *Pass between two sections of an old house ruins. Bear left at the Y.*

6.59 *Pass a trail on your left that goes uphill.*

This trail may become part of the designated bike trail.

6.80 *At a large, messy intersection where several roads and trails meet, continue straight.*

6.97 *At a Y, go right. The left goes uphill slightly, the right goes downhill.*

7.05 *Bear left at a Y, going slightly uphill. Continue with Potake Pond on your right.*

7.51 *Turn left at a Y, about halfway up Potake Pond. Climb.*

8.00 *Pass a trail on your left and immediately afterward arrive at a Y. Go left, between some orange-blazed boulders on the trail. Head downhill slightly.*

8.28 *At a four-way intersection, go straight.*

Shepherd Lake becomes visible during sparse foliage. Soon the lake will appear on your right.

9.05 *Arrive at the beach area. Turn left at the entrance booth, follow Shepherd Lake Road back to Skylands, hit Morris Avenue, and continue toward your car on the road you drove in on.*

10.35 *Arrive at parking lot C.*

Information

Ringwood State Park
Box 1304, Ringwood, NJ 07456
973-962-7031 or 973-962-7047

Bicycle Repair Services

Town Cycle
1468 Union Valley Road, West Milford, NJ
973-728-8878

Spokes
16 Lafayette Avenue, Suffern, NY
914-357-8125

2
Ramapo Mountain State Forest

Location: *Oakland Township, Bergen County; Boro of Wanaque, Passaic County*
Distance: *6.55 miles, with additional legal dirt trails*
Terrain: *Hilly*
Surface: *Dirt and paved roads*
Maps: *NYNJTC North Jersey Trails, Eastern Portion, Trail Map #22*
Highlights: *Quiet roads for beginning cyclists; scenic view of Manhattan skyline; several wooded roads and side trails*

Although strictly a beginner or "off-day" ride, Ramapo Mountain State Forest also currently draws very advanced riders, who roam the peripheral trails from the Barbara Drive parking area, just south of I-287, all the way to Ringwood State Park via the Cannonball Trail or (illegally) the Tenneco gas pipeline. The state trails plan, as of this writing still in process, will determine whether these surrounding trails will become legal for bikers. Management has realized that the user group is expanding (the park office gets 150 calls a week from bikers, 2 from hikers), proactive, and, most of all, well financed. So the plan will be more generous than most mountain bikers might have dared to hope, including a trail link between Ramapo and Ringwood either on sections of the Cannonball Trail, on the pipeline, or on both. You'll have the opportunity to at least look at the pipeline from Ramapo State Forest, but right now it's technically off-limits. Restrictions will also be placed on the little singletracks such as the Hoeferlin, Lookout, and possibly the Todd Trails to the east of Ramapo Lake. While it's true that these trails can't bear the continued high impact they're getting now (by merit of their popularity with both bikers and hikers), unfortunately the most pressing issue determining their closure is not their preservation, but the

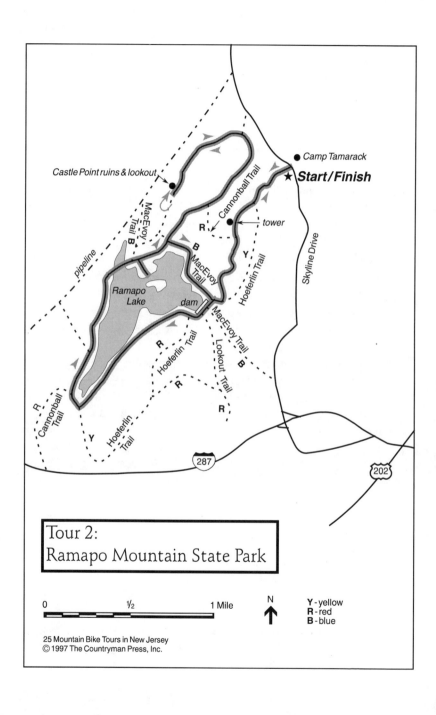

Camp Tamarack

★ **Start/Finish**

Castle Point ruins & lookout

MacEvoy Trail **B**

pipeline

Cannonball Trail

R

tower

Y

Hoeferlin Trail

Skyline Drive

Ramapo Lake

MacEvoy Trail

dam

MacEvoy Trail **B**

R

Hoeferlin Trail

Lookout Trail

R

R

R
Cannonball Trail

Y

Hoeferlin Trail

287

202

Tour 2:
Ramapo Mountain State Park

0   ½   1 Mile

N

Y - yellow
R - red
B - blue

25 Mountain Bike Tours in New Jersey
© 1997 The Countryman Press, Inc.

increased difficulty for rescuers in the event of injury and the resulting burden on the underfunded, understaffed park system.

The recommended North Jersey trail map carries an interesting history of the forest and trail development in general, but it also erroneously states that access to Ramapo Mountain State Forest is by foot only, and "trail bikes" are not allowed. In fact, motorized trail bikes are not permitted, but mountain bikes are legal as of this writing. (This situation may change with the completion of the state trails plan.)

To reach this park, take I-287 to the exit marked Skyline Drive (County Route 91) and travel north. Go past the lower entrance to the forest on your left at 0.3 mile, and continue uphill another 1.1 miles. Park on the left, across Skyline Drive from Camp Tamarack (Boy Scouts of America).

0.00 *Head through the gate and watch out for pedestrians. This is a busy place. Go downhill on broken pavement. Several dirt trails depart from this road, including a section of the yellow Hoeferlin Trail, which may be closed to bikes. Continue.*

0.55 *Pass an observation tower on your right.*

1.20 *Arrive at Ramapo Lake and the dam. There's a portable rest room here. Keeping the lake to your right, continue as the road becomes broken stone and gravel, bearing right at the intersections.*

Some of these dirt side trails may be legal in the future.

2.50 *Cross the bridge at the northwest end of the lake.*

2.60 *Go straight, next to the lake. The MacEvoy Trail, to your left (blue), climbs to the pipeline. Check the trail's legality and that of the pipeline before proceeding; if either is off-limits at the time you read this, signs will be posted here.*

2.70 *Turn right onto a dirt path, which heads out to a dead end over the lake.*

This is the best picnic spot on the tour with the exception of Castle Point, which has a view of Manhattan and Wanaque.

Return to the road and turn right.

3.10 *Between two large concrete pillars, turn left and begin the climb to Castle Point.*

3.90 *Pass the gatehouse (occupied) and continue.*

4.10 *Arrive at a ruins.*

Secure your bike and continue on foot, or bring your bike if you have to, a little way beyond the ruin to a lookout. You can see the New York skyline to the east, the Wanaque Reservoir to the west.

Return the way you came.

As you're coming down the hill, almost at the bottom on your left you'll see the red-marked Cannonball Trail. This is a difficult trail for the inexperienced rider, and by the time you read this, the Cannonball may well be illegal, but there's a beautiful spring about 0.1 mile down it. Go check it out on foot if need be.

5.10 *Turn left as you go through the pillars onto the lake road. This is technically the blue MacEvoy Trail.*

5.35 *Turn left at the dam and ascend on the road.*

6.55 *Arrive at the parking area.*

Information

Ramapo State Forest
c/o Ringwood State Park, Box 1304
Ringwood, NJ 07456
973-962-7031 or 973-962-7047

Bicycle Repair Services

Ridgewood Cycle Shop
35 North Broad Street, Ridgewood, NJ
201-444-2553

Richlyn Bike Shop, Inc.
Allendale, NJ
201-825-0952

Note: As of fall 1998, the following trail was closed until further notice.

3

Pequannock Watershed—
Charlotteburg Reservoir

Location: Newfoundland, Passaic, and Morris Counties
Distance: 5.15 miles, with miles of unexplored, unmapped trails
Terrain: Hilly, with long flats
Surface: Dirt, ballast, single and doubletrack
Maps: Pequannock Watershed Trails Map (free at Echo Lake office),
USGS Newfoundland, Boonton
Highlights: Isolated, unmarked, varied terrain with unlimited opportunities for exploring new trails

The Pequannock Watershed represents one of the state's largest municipally managed natural resources, a varied environment of ponds, streams, forests, ridges, and swamps. Heavily used by the early farming, logging, mining, and ice-harvesting industries, the 35,000-acre watershed is crisscrossed with dirt roads and skid trails. It's virtually unknown to mountain bikers.

Volunteer trail development and marking began soon after the 1974 creation of the Newark Watershed Conservation and Development Corporation. More marking than actual "development" was performed, though. Trails that are currently marked and "maintained" (some of them haven't seen maintenance in years) by the NYNJTC are fair game double- and singletracks. Considerable miles of unmarked trails and roads are open to exploration.

The area has been heavily impacted by ATV use, and you'll occasionally see heaps of household trash. The singletrack trails appear to be seldom used, though, and chances are that except for ATVs on weekends, you won't see a soul. Lack of staffing has contributed to the under-

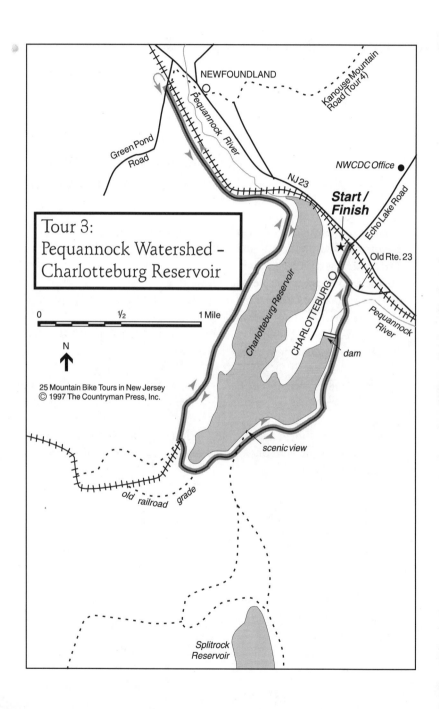

Tour 3:
Pequannock Watershed –
Charlotteburg Reservoir

0   ½   1 Mile

N

25 Mountain Bike Tours in New Jersey
© 1997 The Countryman Press, Inc.

NEWFOUNDLAND

Pequannock River

Green Pond Road

Kanouse Mountain Road (Tour 4)

NWCDC Office

NJ 23

Start / Finish

Echo Lake Road

Old Rte. 23

Charlotteburg Reservoir

CHARLOTTEBURG

Pequannock River

dam

scenic view

old railroad grade

Splitrock Reservoir

management of this resource. The watershed staff is very helpful and friendly, and they know the area better than anyone else. Even they, however, are amazed at the miles and variety of the dirt road network, and ultimately you have to rely on yourself.

Bicyclists, hikers, hunters, anglers, and equestrians are allowed access to the area by permit. At this time the price of a seasonal day-use permit is $8. Some trails are restricted, and management asks that cyclists stay off of the Highlands Trail in particular. Get your permit at the Echo Lake office. From Butler, take NJ 23 and head west about 6 miles to Echo Lake Road, which is 1 mile or so east of Newfoundland. Turn right onto Echo Lake Road and look for the office on your left within 1 mile. Be sure to request a trail map (not the inferior hunting map) along with your permit, although the maps are of little practical use at this time. For navigation purposes the conference map is the handiest; it doesn't cover the Charlotteburg area, but it's necessary for exploring the watershed north of Newfoundland. County maps are good for distance touring that may involve road miles, and the USGS Boonton map is also useful. Then again, you may not care where you are, in which case you're never lost. But beware: Some of these trails seem endless. Come prepared.

Leave the watershed office, go straight back across NJ 23, and park in the lot next to the railroad tracks and NJ 23. Quite a few commuters use this lot.

0.00 *Get on your bike here, and head south on the paved road next to the parking lot—Old Route 23, an extension of Echo Lake Road.*

0.20 *Pass a gate to your right, and bear left as the road heads southeast.*

There's also a house on your right, and the watershed maintenance buildings are here.

0.25 *Pass another gate on your right.*

This paved service road is open to bikes, and you can take a short scenic ride on it out to the Charlotteburg Dam.

Continue straight on Old Route 23.

0.33 *Directly across from a private residence, turn right through a gate (large concrete blocks on each side discourage*

Charlotteburg Reservoir Outlet

motorized vehicle entry). You're now on a wide dirt road.

0.45 *Cross the outlet of Charlotteburg Reservoir (the Pequannock River). Continue on the dirt road, passing several other roads and trails.*

1.65 *Reach a four-way intersection. The road to the right goes down to a scenic view of the reservoir (0.2 mile). The left*

turn goes to Splitrock Reservoir. Go straight.

The Splitrock trails are some of the finest anywhere, but at this time the watershed manager (Jersey City) has a "no public use" policy. It's uncertain where the Pequannock boundaries are, posting is poor, and the roads (miles upon miles) are heavily impacted by ATV use. If you venture into the area, observe the postings, and carry the USGS Boonton map, which shows the main roads.

1.95 *At a sweeping turn to the left, bear right onto a rough trail that heads toward the south end of the reservoir. This trail then goes uphill on a loose, rocky surface.*

2.50 *Bear right. The trail levels as it joins an old railbed. As you follow the railroad right-of-way, you'll see several trails on each side of the bed. Continue straight.*

3.00 *Follow beside an intact (abandoned) track.*

5.15 *Arrive at Green Pond Road; across is the Newfoundland Train Station. To your right and then south on NJ 23 are a deli, phone, and several stores. Riding on the shoulder of NJ 23 is hectic during rush hour. You can return the way you came, or cross over the highway here to connect with the Bearfort Mountain tour via Kanouse Mountain Road. See the directions at the beginning of Tour 4.*

Information

NWCDC
PO Box 319, Newfoundland, NJ 07435
201-697-2850

Bicycle Repair Services

Town Cycle
1468 Union Valley Road, West Milford, NJ
201-728-8878

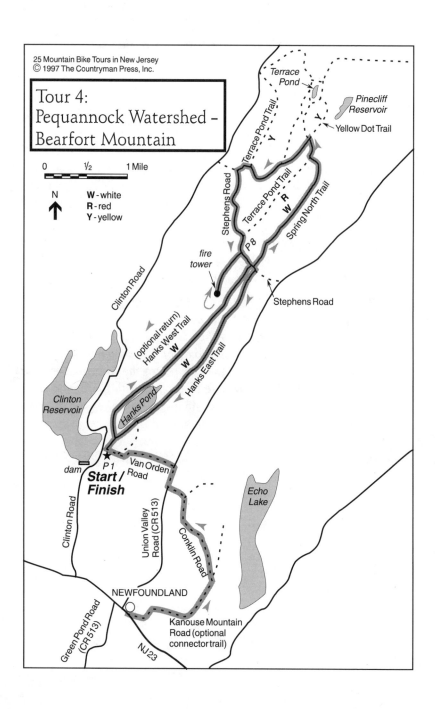

25 Mountain Bike Tours in New Jersey
© 1997 The Countryman Press, Inc.

Tour 4: Pequannock Watershed – Bearfort Mountain

0   ½   1 Mile

N

W - white
R - red
Y - yellow

Terrace Pond

Pinecliff Reservoir

Terrace Pond Trail

Y

Yellow Dot Trail

Stephens Road

Terrace Pond Trail

R
W

P 8

Spring North Trail

fire tower

Stephens Road

(optional return) Hanks West Trail

W

W

Hanks East Trail

Clinton Reservoir

Hanks Pond

dam

P 1

Start / Finish

Van Orden Road

Clinton Road

Clinton Road

Union Valley Road (CR 513)

Conklin Road

Echo Lake

NEWFOUNDLAND

Green Pond Road (CR 513)

Kanouse Mountain Road (optional connector trail)

NJ 23

Note: As of fall 1998, the following trail was closed until further notice.

4

Pequannock Watershed
—Bearfort Mountain

Location: West Milford Township, Passaic and Morris Counties
Distance: 9.85 miles
Terrain: Rocky, hilly
Surface: Rocky, muddy doubletrack trails
Maps: Pequannock Watershed Trails Map (free at Echo Lake office), USGS Newfoundland, NYNJTC North Jersey Trails, Western Portion, trail map #21
Highlights: Miles of interconnecting trails, many of them legal single-track; proximity to Wawayanda State Park and facilities

Bearfort Mountain is another excellent spot that's open to mountain bikers—they just don't realize it. It's part of the Pequannock Watershed, a large natural area with the potential for extended touring. If you look at either the USGS or the NYNJTC map, you'll see how easily you can use the trails in the watershed to access those of Wawayanda State Park to the north (see Tour 5) as well as the many unnamed watershed trails between Echo Lake and the Canistear Reservoir to the west. A comprehensive inventory of the entire trail system doesn't exist and probably never will. Fortunately, though, the Bearfort trails have been marked and maintained by the NYNJTC, making for easy navigation on the Bearfort Ridge and north.

However, there are some sensitive trails on Bearfort that can't bear the impact of heavy cycling use, especially the fire tower trails; you're hereby encouraged to avoid them. Other parts of the ridge are either too steep or too rocky to ride. But the majority of doubletrack trails described here—which see little use, even by hikers—were built as fire or access roads and can take significant impact. As a general rule of thumb, until watershed management plans can identify and mark the area's sensitive trails, stay off any trail that doesn't already show signs of significant impact.

You'll need a day-use permit to ride at Bearfort. The area is managed by the Newark Watershed Conservation and Development Corporation, and you can pick up a permit (and map) at its Echo Lake office. From Butler, take NJ 23 and head west about 6 miles to Echo Lake Road; turn north and look for the office on your left within 1 mile.

There are several ways to begin the ride itself. For one, park at the Clinton Reservoir. From there, return to NJ 23 and head northwest to County Route 513 (Union Valley Road); 1.75 miles north on CR 513 turn left onto Van Orden Road. Then just follow Van Orden Road 1 mile to the reservoir and park.

Or you can add this tour to the Charlotteburg Reservoir ride by following Kanouse Road from Newfoundland to Van Orden Road (3 miles), following the directions below. If you're not planning to do both tours, though, forget Kanouse Road—it's not that exciting. Better to spend your time in Bearfort. Also, riding the two tours back-to-back can amount to some strenuous mileage if you're exploring a bit.

Kanouse Mountain Road Connector: Charlotteburg and Bearfort Mountain Tours

From Newfoundland—just south of the intersection of NJ 23 and Green Pond Road (CR 513)—find Kanouse Mountain Road by bearing northeast from town. Only two other roads bear north, and both are dead ends. You'll come upon an old, open watershed gate. With a permit, you can park anywhere along here if you want. Don't try to drive this road, but do take the time to explore on and off it with your bike. There are several miles of side trails.

0.00 *Set your cyclometer at the entrance to watershed property. As soon as you enter, the road splits. Bear right, crossing Kanouse Brook immediately.*

> The brook washes over the road in periods of high water. Keep your speed up to stay dry! Travel generally uphill. The dirt road is full of rocks and potholes.

Hanks Pond

0.80 Turn left off Kanouse Road onto another dirt road (Conklin Road). You go between two cement columns here and descend slightly.

1.80 At a Y, bear left.

2.00 Arrive at Union Valley Road (CR 513) and turn right.

2.25 Turn left onto Van Orden Road. Go uphill.

3.20 Arrive at Clinton Road.

There are several legal parking areas in the vicinity, none of which is marked. It's worth the time to go left here and take a look at the dam at the south end of the Clinton Reservoir. This is a good place to rest if there's a breeze—though early in the season the blackflies will keep you on your bike.

At the intersection of Van Orden and Clinton Roads, there's a cable gate across a woods road. This is the Hanks Pond Trail (Hanks West on the NYNJTC map).

There are several legal parking areas here.

Bearfort Mountain Tour

0.00 *From the intersection of Van Orden and Clinton Roads, follow the Hanks West Trail north.*

0.20 *At a Y, you'll see three white dots to the right, and three blue dots to the left. Go left.*

Momentarily, you'll see Hanks Pond on your right. Ride right along the edge of Hanks Pond.

This trail is rocky, wet, and poorly maintained. There's plenty of mud in season. Sure would be nice to have front suspension here.

1.60 *Pass the Highlands Trail (off-limits).*

2.58 *At Stephens Road, turn right, go 200 feet, then turn left onto the Spring North Trail, a nice grassy doubletrack. Climb. The trail levels out at about 1200 feet.*

3.88 *As you turn northwest with the trail, there's a steep, rocky descent. Be careful. Pass a few trails on your left, including the Highlands Trail (newly constructed and cairned), and the blue trail.*

4.00 *You may have to make some short detours through a wetland, depending on the time of year. Following the wet area, you'll see the obscure (red) Terrace Pond Trail as it heads southwest. Go up a steep, rocky hill, bearing right on the Terrace Pond Trail for a short time.*

4.20 *At a T, the Yellow Dot Trail heads right.*

This detour leads to a view over the Pinecliff Reservoir. The ride is nice, but the view isn't worth the trip if the leaves are out.

Go left here, staying on the main trail. There are several confusing side trails here, none of which conform to the park map.

5.10 *Where the Terrace Pond South Trail turns north toward Bearfort Waters, bear left toward Stephens Road.*

5.30 *Turn left on Stephens Road.*

6.25 *At gate P8, turn right and climb toward the fire tower.*

6.60 *Arrive at the fire tower.*

Excellent views of the watershed are available here, as well as a few picnic tables.

Descend back to Stephens Road.

6.95 *Turn right on Stephens Road.*

7.15 *Pass the Hanks West trail on your right.*

If you've had enough, you can return to your point of origin here, but if you'd like to see another trail, continue on Stephens Road.

7.25 *Pass the Spring North Trail on your left.*

7.35 *Turn right onto the Hanks East Trail, a somewhat rockier, hillier version of Hanks West.*

9.85 *Arrive at gate P1 and your point of departure.*

Information

NWCDC
PO Box 319, Newfoundland, NJ 07435
973-697-2850

Bicycle Repair Services

Town Cycle
1468 Union Valley Road, West Milford, NJ
973-728-8878

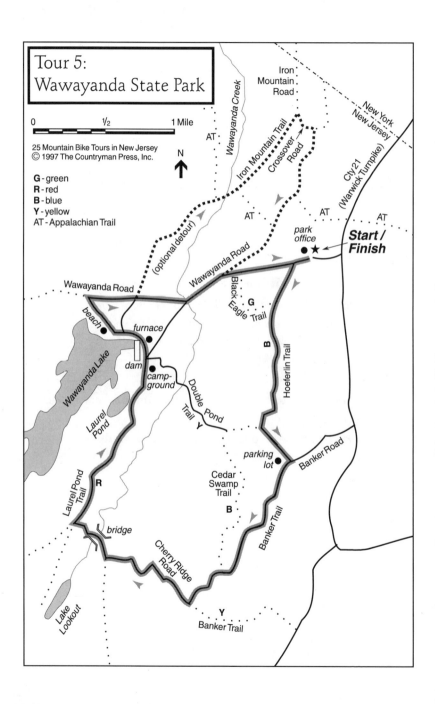

Tour 5:
Wawayanda State Park

0   ½   1 Mile

25 Mountain Bike Tours in New Jersey
© 1997 The Countryman Press, Inc.

N

G - green
R - red
B - blue
Y - yellow
AT - Appalachian Trail

Iron
Mountain
Road

New York
New Jersey

Wawayanda Creek

Iron Mountain Trail

Crossover Road

Cty 21 (Wanwick Turnpike)

AT

AT

AT

AT

(optional detour)

Wawayanda Road

park office

*Start /
Finish*

★

Wawayanda Road

Black Eagle Trail

G

B

Hoeferlin Trail

beach

furnace

dam

*camp-
ground*

Wawayanda Lake

Laurel Pond

Double Pond Trail

Y

Banker Road

parking lot

Cedar
Swamp
Trail

B

Laurel Pond Trail

R

Banker Trail

bridge

Cherry Ridge Road

Lake
Lookout

Y

Banker Trail

5
Wawayanda State Park

Location: *Highland Lakes Township, Sussex County, access from Warwick, New York*
Distance: *9.8-mile loop, 5.4-mile detour, more mileage available*
Terrain: *Rocky, hilly*
Surface: *Dirt and gravel roads to variable-terrain singletrack*
Maps: *Wawayanda State Park, State Park Service map (free); NYNJTC North Jersey Trails, Trail Map #21*
Highlights: *Single- and doubletrack riding on varied terrain suitable to intermediate and advanced riders; many beginner trails; swimming, fishing, boating; group camping; natural areas; picnic area; accessibility for people with disabilities*

With a combination of singletrack, carriage road, swamp, rhododendron forest, and back roads, Wawayanda is one of the most attractive and biker-friendly state parks in New Jersey. There's a considerable black bear population in the park, along with a variety of other wildlife. And with activities ranging from water sports in 255-acre Wawayanda Lake to camping, hiking, and cycling in the park's 13,000 acres, Wawayanda is aptly described as an "oasis for nature and recreation" by the state's division of parks and forestry.

Wawayanda was at one time (1845–1890) the site of a mining village developed by the family of Oliver Ames, who built a blast furnace (which you'll see) and dammed the outlet of what is now Wawayanda Lake. The original 5600-acre Wawayanda Furnace Property is still part of the park. A large section of the southwestern parkland—Bearfort Mountain—was originally the land of another ironmaster, Abram S. Hewitt of Ringwood fame (see Tour 17). It appears that mountain bikers have benefited considerably from the country's early iron industry.

The park has many more trails and through roads available to cyclists than are described in this tour. Several days of touring are possible without repetition. You can use some of the park's trails as well as a bike path along Wawayanda Road between the park office and the lake. The outlying areas of Bearfort Mountain and Wawayanda Hemlock Ravine are too steep for biking, although a different section of the Bearfort Mountain area is ridable; it's described in Tour 3, the Pequannock Watershed. Certain trails in the park are closed to bikes, and these are in the process of being identified.

This tour lends itself to a daylong outing, which can culminate conveniently in a swim or picnic at the lake, about 10 miles in. There's a small food concession there, as well as facilities for cookouts. You can ride the remaining few miles either on Wawayanda Road (a mellow, 35 mph road and bikeway) or through the woods on the Iron Mountain Trail.

The park is located in Highland Lakes, New Jersey, between West Milford, New Jersey, and Warwick, New York, on County Route 21 (the Warwick Turnpike). From North Jersey—Sussex, Morris, and Passaic Counties—Warwick can be reached by taking CR 23 to CR 94. From the north reach Warwick by taking I-84 to NY 17 east, then heading south on CR 94. Either way, from Warwick go 3 miles southwest on CR 94 (toward New Milford) and turn left onto CR 21. After 2.9 miles turn into the park entrance (on your right).

You can park outside the main office. There's no need to go through the toll and pay for lake-area parking. (If you arrive after 4 PM, entry to the entire area is free.) Maps, information, rest rooms, and a telephone are available at the staffed office. There's no charge for biking at this time.

The trail is a short distance from the office, about halfway between it and the toll houses, on the left. Look carefully for the inconspicuous trailhead and its sign that reads WM. HOEFERLIN TRAIL (BLUE).

0.00 *Start, going uphill, then leveling out. The trail is rocky but easily negotiated. Marking is fair.*

0.50 *At an intersection with the Black Eagle Trail (green on white), go diagonally across, staying on the blue. Marking is good.*

The trail is rocky, rooty, and rarely level, but it's suited to intermediate riders.

1.80 *At a T, turn left onto the Double Pond Trail (yellow). Marking*

is poor. This area is low and very muddy after rain or in spring. Stay to the side.

2.20 At the Banker Trail parking area, bear right, continuing on Banker Trail.

3.80 At Cherry Ridge Road, go right.

4.40 Cross a shallow creek where the road is washed out.

4.60 Cross an intact bridge over the Lake Lookout outlet. Watch carefully on your right for the Laurel Pond Trail (no marking).

4.80 Turn right onto the Laurel Pond Trail. Your only cue is a tall, elegant stand of red pine trees (the bark is reddish brown). This is a singletrack, narrow but well defined, heading slightly uphill.

5.10 The trail, heavily marked in red, splits. Go left. This appears to be a re-marking from the original yellow.

5.40 The trail that split off at 5.1 miles (red) rejoins from the right.

5.80 Cross a small plank bridge.

5.90 At a T, turn left.

6.10 Cross a bridge over a small Wawayanda outlet creek. Climb easily.

6.60 Go through a barrier gate and into the camping area. Bear left.

6.65 Reach a five-way intersection.

The big stone structure that you see to your right is what remains of the old blast furnace of the Wawayanda ironworks.

Go up the hill, leaving the furnace directly to your right.

6.75 Arrive at Wawayanda Lake. Bear right. There's a low dam to your left.

7.00 Pass through the boating area. Continue straight.

7.30 Arrive at the public beach and picnic area. The lake is large and scenic, a nice place to rest. As you leave the beach, follow Wawayanda Road. It's 2.5 miles back to the main entrance and your car.

If you wish to add more mileage, follow the Iron Mountain Road (blue) back to the main gate in a route that will add 4 more miles.

9.80 Arrive back at the parking lot.

Iron Mountain Detour

0.00 Leave Wawayanda Lake beach area, turning right onto Wawayanda Road.

0.60 Go left onto the Iron Mountain Trail (not marked); it's a wide doubletrack (or jeep trail). If you pass the GROUP CAMPING sign you've gone too far. Continue on this trail.

There are many legal singletracks in this area.

2.60 Bear right onto Crossover Road (not marked).

The Iron Mountain Trail bears left here to leave the park, indicated by a small sign.

2.95 Bear right at a Y. (The left goes out of the park.)

4.60 Turn left onto Wawayanda Road.

5.40 Arrive at the park entrance and your car.

If you include the Iron Mountain Trail, your total trip distance is 12.7 miles.

Information

Wawayanda State Park
PO Box 198, Highland Lakes, NJ
973-853-4462

Bicycle Repair Services

Town Cycle
1468 Union Valley Road, West Milford, NJ
973-728-8878

6

Mahlon Dickerson Reservation

Location: *Jefferson Township, Morris County*
Distance: *North loop, 5.6 miles; south loop, 6.5 miles*
Terrain: *Expert singletrack. Extremely rocky hills and flats with 2-mile railbed*
Surface: *Wide trails with challenging mixtures: cinder, gravel mixed with loose rock, bedrock, ruts, and slop at marsh and pond outlets*
Maps: *Mahlon Dickerson Reservation park commission pocket map (free); USGS Dover; Franklin, Newton East (helpful for reference only)*
Highlights: *Multiuse park with hiking, legal singletrack biking, equestrian trails, picnic tables and shelters; rest rooms, phones; RV and tent camping areas, lean-tos; 3042 wooded acres*

Situated in the northernmost, central point of the county, this park is the largest in the Morris County system. It has a quiet and removed atmosphere, in contrast to the Patriots' Path and Lewis Morris Park (Tours 8 and 7), two other prominent mountain biking destinations nearby also maintained by the county. The reason for Dickerson's relatively low level of use is the advanced level of riding difficulty. These are primarily expert trails, with few stretches of the fast, bare flats found in local parks. The police have reported many injuries here (though most were connected to the park's races, which are no longer conducted).

Since the trails see little midweek use until after working hours, prepare accordingly for repair, first aid, and liquids. (Water is available at the picnic area.) In addition to the described route, many more miles of hilly, challenging trails can be found far from the road. Ride carefully and, when possible, ride with a partner. If you're one who tempts fate by being only an occasional helmet user, this is an important place to use one.

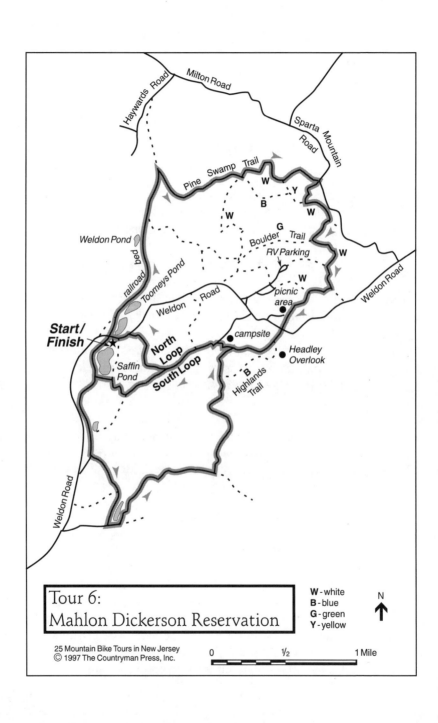

Haywards Road
Milton Road
Sparta Mountain Road
Pine Swamp Trail
W
Y
B
W
W
W
G Boulder Trail
RV Parking
W
W
picnic area
Weldon Pond
railroad bed
Toomeys Pond
Weldon Road
Weldon Road
campsite
Headley Overlook
Start/ Finish
North Loop
Saffin Pond
South Loop
B Highlands Trail
Weldon Road

Tour 6:
Mahlon Dickerson Reservation

25 Mountain Bike Tours in New Jersey
© 1997 The Countryman Press, Inc.

W - white
B - blue
G - green
Y - yellow

N

0   ½   1 Mile

To reach the park (directions are also found on the trail map that's distributed at most Morris County bike shops), take I-80 to the exit for NJ 15 North. (If you're getting off I-287, take I-80 West to this exit.) Go 5 miles and get off at the Weldon Road exit. Follow Weldon Road east for 3.5 miles to the Saffin Pond Parking Area. Begin here. You'll find a telephone and an information board with maps at this lot. There's no on-site management and no fee for day use. Park police regularly patrol the facilities, but you probably won't see them on the trails.

The two loops (north and south) described here are the most popular in this park. They will provide a rigorous tour with an overview of the perimeter trails. Many more legal singletrack trails are contained within the North Loop, which climbs to 1395 feet, the highest point in Morris County.

The North Loop

0.00 *From the west end of the parking lot, cross Weldon Road onto the (circa-1865) railbed, go through the gate, and head north over a gravel surface, passing Toomeys Pond on your right.*

Bike trail markers are posted sporadically. There are no ties, and you ride on an improved but poorly maintained gravel-over-ballast surface. Heavy rutting retains water for days after a rainfall. Illegal ATVs worsen potholing and rutting.

0.75 *Pass Weldon Pond.*

1.00 *Pass a singletrack that leaves your trail at about a 120-degree angle.*

1.25 *Arrive at an intersection. The trail to the left is private. Going straight ahead on the railbed would take you to Haywards Road and a dead end. There are bridle path markers here. Go right.*

The barrier gate at Haywards Road is poorly maintained, and you may thus encounter all-terrain vehicles on the railbed. After you turn off here, however, the trail is rugged and inaccessible even to ATVs. Blowdowns, rocks, and overspill from the west-lying Pine Swamp makes this a particularly interesting, potentially sloppy, and technically demanding section.

Tim Gifford: In No Time Flat

1.90 *At a Y, turn left. This is the white-marked Pine Swamp Trail. Horse and bike markers appear only on your right.*

Follow the east shoulder of Pine Swamp (headwaters of the Wallkill River) through a varied, attractive hardwood and hemlock forest at an elevation of 1250 feet—high for this part of New Jersey.

2.30 *At an intersection, bear left, staying on white. A yellow-marked trail departs to your right.*

2.60 *At a junction, a paved road (Sparta Mountain Road) appears straight ahead. Turn right before you reach the road, staying on the white trail. Follow downhill and cross a wooden footbridge, bearing right. This is a short section of the Highlands Trail.*

2.80 *Bear left to stay on the white trail. The yellow trail goes to the right.*

2.90 *Go right at a Y. An unmarked trail to the left leads to the road. Following the white markers, go over a tiny, single-plank bridge through a rocky area.*

3.05 *Go right at a T.*

3.15 *Cross a northeast-flowing brook (headwaters of the Rockaway River) and continue up a steep hill. The trail splits here, and you can go either way, but markers follow the right side. Within a short distance, the trail reconnects.*

3.25 *At a T, go left, staying on the white trail. The green-marked Boulder Trail goes right.*

3.55 *Go left at another T. The RV parking area is to your right; a knoll just northeast of you is 1250 feet in elevation. White and blue markers appear to your left. Go downhill, an easy, short descent.*

3.65 *At a T, go right and ascend toward the picnic area.*

3.85 *Turn left at the intersection of the Pine Swamp Trail, toward the picnic area. Go through the picnic area (bathrooms and a water pump here), and bear left into the woods just past*

the signboard. This takes you toward the road and Headley
Overlook.

4.15 Cross Weldon Road.

4.30 Go straight at a Y.

Headley Overlook is to your left. The trail to the overlook is off-
limits to bikes. If it's a clear day, walk up for a look.

4.45 Bear right at a Y. To your left is the south entrance trail to
Headley Overlook.

4.60 Turn left within view of the campsite parking area, before
reaching the pavement, onto an unmarked rocky singletrack.
Follow downhill, cross a small creek, then climb.

4.80 Bear left at a Y. The trail to your right goes to Weldon Road.

5.05 Go right. This fast, nice trail brings you out to Weldon Road.

5.50 Turn left on Weldon Road.

5.60 The Saffin Pond parking area is on your left.

The South Loop

0.00 From the Saffin Pond parking lot, go west and then turn
immediately south onto the gravel railbed. Go past Saffin
Pond, which is to your left.

0.32 Go straight.

There's a path across the south end of the lake here, with a picnic area. You'll be returning from that direction.

0.85 Turn left off the railbed.

A wetland and pond will soon appear to your left. Marking
tends to be poor through here.

1.42 Turn left when you hit the paved road. Cross the dam at the
south end of the pond.

1.50 Turn left onto the dirt trail, which soon ascends.

This trail is technically difficult, especially when wet.

2.30 At the top of a hill, turn left. A dirt road goes straight here
and leaves the reservation. Cruise for a while until you hit a

slop area, which can be very muddy in the spring, requiring a fair portage. Following is a steep incline.

3.00 *At the top of a rise, the blue Highlands Trail markers go to the right to Headley Overlook. This is a sensitive trail that should not be ridden.*

3.20 *Turn left. If you've already done the North Loop, you've been here before. Go downhill until you see the campsite road, but don't go into the campsite.*

3.35 *Turn left onto an unmarked, rocky singletrack. Cross a small creek, then climb.*

3.70 *Bear left at a Y.*

3.98 *At another Y, bear right.*

There are blue Highlands Trail markers on each side of the Y at this point. This section is downhill and rocky.

4.20 *Arrive at the lake and go straight. Don't take the blue trail to your right here, which goes along the lake's edge; it's very rough. Cross the dam at the south end of Saffin Pond.*

4.30 *Turn right onto the railbed.*

4.60 *Arrive at the parking area.*

Information

Mahlon Dickerson Reservation
Morris County Parks Commission
PO Box 1295, Morristown, NJ 07062-1295
201-326-7600

Park police: 911; 201-326-7632

Bicycle Repair Services

Bicycle Outlet
Route 15, Pathmark Center, Lake Hopatcong, NJ
973-663-1935

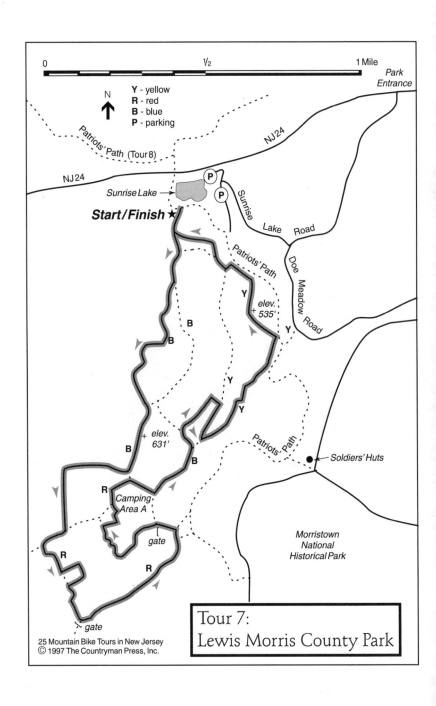

0   ½   1 Mile

Y - yellow
R - red
B - blue
P - parking

N

Park Entrance

Patriots' Path (Tour 8)

NJ 24

NJ 24

Sunrise Lake

P

P

Sunrise Lake Road

Start/Finish ★

Patriots' Path

Doe Meadow Road

Y

elev. +535'

B

Y

B

Y

Y

elev. +631'

B

Patriots' Path

B

Soldiers' Huts

R

Camping Area A

R

gate

Morristown National Historical Park

R

R

gate

25 Mountain Bike Tours in New Jersey
© 1997 The Countryman Press, Inc.

Tour 7:
Lewis Morris County Park

7

Lewis Morris County Park

Location: *Morristown, Morris County*
Distance: *4.23 miles; joins with 18.8-mile Patriots' Path*
Terrain: *Hilly*
Surface: *Dirt singletrack trails*
Maps: *Lewis Morris County Park Commission map (free)*
Highlights: *Camping, picnic shelters; boating, swimming; equestrian trails; Morristown National Historic Park; Frelinghuysen Arboretum (headquarters, Morris County Park Commission)*

This jewel in the Morris County Park Commission's system was the first to open, in 1958. Among its attractions is the county's usual friendliness toward multiple users, a feature that has enamored the park to many out-of-town riders. NORBA-sanctioned races are held here regularly, and the trail system is a combination of gentle to moderately demanding hilly dirt singletracks.

There's plenty for a family to do here, too, which can justify an outing if your group contains nonriders. Aside from boating, swimming, picnicking, and hiking, there's a large play area for children, and camping is allowed. There's also a par course, a fitness circuit, and a few softball fields.

Across NJ 24, but otherwise connected to this park, is the Patriots' Path (see Tour 8), an extensive linear trail system adequate for riders of most ability levels beyond rank beginner.

Lewis Morris Park itself, though much easier than the county's more demanding ATB mecca, Mahlon Dickerson Reservation (Tour 6), does have its share of technical terrain and must rank somewhere in the intermediate ability range. There aren't nearly as many rocks here as you'll find in Dickerson, however—a most welcoming feature for some purely recreational riders. But you'll also find a lot more public use here, particularly on nice weekend days, and you're asked to avoid race routes when events are scheduled. Races don't last all day, though, and if you do arrive in the midst of one you can either enter, watch, or go ride on the Patriots' Path. Call ahead for details if you're planning a visit (order a map while you're doing so).

Anybody can enter the races, incidentally, with the purchase of a 1-day or annual NORBA license and the payment of a race fee. Categories are designed to fit your ability level, and you'll quickly find out where you fit in once you do a few loops with a cadre of seasoned riders.

To reach Lewis Morris Park from I-287, take exit 35 and head west into Morristown on NJ 24 (between I-287 and Morristown this road may be identified as NJ 124). Continue through town, around the village green. About 3.5 miles from I-287, the park entrance will appear on your left. Follow signs to the Sunrise Lake Parking Area.

A signboard posts a comprehensive list of rules and regulations, as well as a map. To your left as you face this signboard is a gated park access road. Proceed through the gate, where signs say no outlet and authorized vehicles only. You can ride or walk through this stretch, but if you ride, watch out for pedestrians. Head downhill and through a small picnic area. You'll see a softball diamond to your right. Pick up the blue equestrian markers and brown Patriots' Path markers as you cross the outlet creek of Sunrise Lake, which is to your right. As you approach the lake you'll see yellow bike trail signs. Go straight on a wide gravel singletrack. The Patriots' Path goes to the right and crosses NJ 24. (Another section of it heads south from this point, along the path you came in on, and turns into the Soldier Hut Trail in Morristown National Historic Park. That area is closed to bikes.)

0.00 *Where the Patriots' Path goes to the right, you go straight on a gravel doubletrack. The trail heads uphill.*

0.13 *Bear right at a T. There are blue paint blazes on the trees here.*

0.23 *At a Y, bear right, following blue markers.*

The terrain levels. This is still a slightly hilly but fast dirt trail. The area is heavily forested; you may see deer.

0.70 *Bear right at another T. Climb a 631-foot rise and head downhill.*

0.90 At a T, go right. (Bikes are also permitted on the trail to the left here.) The trail you're on will take you to the park boundary, then veer south at about a 90-degree angle.

1.11 Cross a creek and head uphill.

1.26 At a T, go right on a trail marked in red. Go downhill through a sweeping curve.

1.43 Pass an unmarked trail on the right.

1.60 Cross a creek and a small wooden bridge. Follow uphill gently.

1.70 Enter a parking lot, bearing left through a gate consisting of two steel posts and a chain. Continue on a single-lane dirt road that bends northward. The trails to the right lead to the Morristown National Historic Park (off-limits to bikes).

2.18 Turn left off the road here, going through a chained gate (the road you're leaving at this point heads directly north to the blue trail).

2.40 Turn right at a T and enter camping area A. Here there's a water pump, several tent platforms, and a latrine. Continue on the red trail. Marking is poor.

2.60 Arrive at a signboard. Turn right and go uphill, off the red and onto the blue trail.

2.70 At a T, bear left, staying on the blue trail. Following bike trail markers, go through a gate that says PEDESTRIANS ONLY. This trail is open to bikes. Come down the hill on the blue trail.

2.95 Go left, off the blue trail.

3.00 Go right, uphill, and around to the north. You'll see yellow blazes along here.

3.13 Join the yellow trail, bearing right.

3.26 Cross a small creek and turn left, following yellow markers.

3.54 Arrive at an open field dotted with a few trees, and bear left. (A continuation of the yellow trail to your right would take you out to Doe Meadow Road.) You'll see white markers along with the yellow here.

3.64 At a Y intersection of the yellow trail and Patriots' Path, bear left on yellow, go uphill to an elevation of 535 feet, then go steeply downhill.

3.88 Crossing a bridge, turn left on yellow.

3.95 At a T, go right and steeply uphill over roots. Bike trail disks appear.

4.13 At another T, you can see Sunrise Lake. Turn right, downhill. Many side trails enter the main trail.

4.23 Return to your starting point near Sunrise Lake.

Information

Morris County Park Commission
PO Box 1295, Morristown, NJ 07962-1295
973-326-7600

Bicycle Repair Services

Marty's Reliable Cycle
173 Speedwell Avenue, Morristown, NJ
973-538-7773

Cycle Center of Denville, Inc.
Main Street and Route 46, Denville, NJ
973-627-2300

8
Patriots' Path

Location: Morristown and Mendham Township, Morris County
Distance: South return trip 8.6 miles; North return trip 10.2 miles;
  total 18.8 miles
Terrain: Hilly
Surface: Dirt, gravel, minimal pavement
Maps: Patriots' Path, Morris County Park Commission (free)
Highlights: Lewis Morris County Park—camping, picnic shelters; boat-
  ing, swimming; equestrian trails; Morristown National Historic Park;
  Frelinghuysen Arboretum (headquarters, Morris County Park
  Commission)

The Patriots' Path is an ever-expanding system of hiking trails, green-strips, and other multiple-use paths. Because of its sensitive location in a heavily populated area along the Whippany, Black, and Raritan Rivers, it's probably the most fussed-over and carefully planned bikeway in New Jersey, along with one of the most user-friendly. But the character of the trail system is surprisingly rural, considering its suburban setting; on an early-summer ride we even saw a white-tailed deer nursing her fawn in the deep skunk cabbage along the Raritan.

The identification and designation of trails in this part of the county is an ongoing process, and the map published by the park commission clearly shows the dedicated (existing) and proposed sections of trail. In conjunction with the National Park Service, county planners are laying out the Patriots' Path proper to eventually reach some 20 miles or more in length. Ultimately it could be part of the longest interconnected trail system in the state, connecting sites of cultural, historic, and natural significance and interest across this area.

Aside from being the popular focal point of the Morris County Park

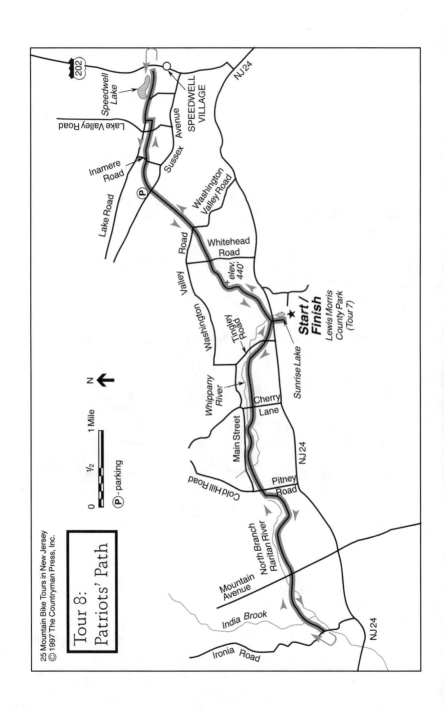

25 Mountain Bike Tours in New Jersey
© 1997 The Countryman Press, Inc.

Tour 8:
Patriots' Path

N ←

0   ½   1 Mile

ℙ - parking

202

Speedwell Lake

Lake Valley Road

Inamere Road

Lake Road

ℙ

Sussex Avenue

SPEEDWELL VILLAGE

NJ 24

Washington Valley Road

Whitehead Road

Valley Road

elev. 440'

Washington

Tingley Road

★ Start / Finish

Lewis Morris County Park (Tour 7)

Sunrise Lake

Whippany River

Cherry Lane

Main Street

NJ 24

Cold Hill Road

Pitney Road

North Branch Raritan River

Mountain Avenue

India Brook

Ironia Road

NJ 24

System, the Patriots' Path serves as a model for greenway design and establishment. It adds considerably to the communities it connects, providing both recreation and transportation as well as preserving open space and creating buffer zones around sensitive environments.

A good way to approach a ride on the Patriots' Path is to combine it with a visit to Lewis Morris County Park, which it adjoins (the parking lot is bigger there, too, although there is Patriots' Path parking off NJ 24 across from Sunrise Lake). To reach Lewis Morris Park from I-287, take exit 35. Go west on NJ 24 through Morristown, circle the village green, and continue until you see the park entrance on the left (a total of 3.5 miles from I-287). About 0.56 mile from the park entrance, turn right onto Sunrise Lake Road, following signs for Sunrise Lake.

Hop on your hill cruiser and head out of the Lewis Morris parking lot on the wide, paved path to the left of the signboard. NO OUTLET and AUTHORIZED VEHICLES ONLY signs are posted here. Go downhill through a small picnic area; you'll see a baseball diamond on your right and, soon, brown Patriots' Path markers as you cross a small creek. Follow these markers to the right across NJ 24 into the Patriots' Path parking area. There's a signboard here with maps. You can also get a trail map at the Morris County Park Commission Cultural Center located on NJ 24, 0.5 mile past the entrance to Lewis Morris County Park, on the left.

Patriots' Path South—Sunrise Lake to Ironia Road

0.00 *Enter the trail system and turn left before crossing a footbridge over the Whippany River. (Signage, despite all my boasting, is poor at this time.)*

If you don't have a map, this trail system will be a mystery. Even with one, you may be uncertain whether you should cross the Whippany River here. (Don't.)

Follow this attractive dirt-and-gravel singletrack along the river, which is on your right.

0.30 *Cross Tingley Road.*

There are a few roots and wet spots through here. You gain elevation in one or two push-up hills, but the trail levels beyond.

> *Go around a private backyard in heavy brush. The trail is good.*

1.30 *Cross Cherry Lane and continue on the trail; it goes behind the Mendham Township Police Station and parallels a nameless tributary of the Whippany River.*

2.40 *Climb uphill slightly and cross Pitney Road (a southerly extension of Cold Hill Road).*

> This height-of-land marks the watershed between the Raritan and Whippany Rivers.

3.40 *Cross Mountain Avenue in front of the Commons at Mendham (a condominium complex). The trail continues over a wide, even, flat surface.*

3.60 *Cross a bridge.*

> This is a pretty, residential area in a rural setting. Pass by a lake and picnic tables at India Brook Park.

4.10 *Gear down before crossing a feeder branch of India Brook, and see if you can cross without getting your feet wet (it's done regularly by little kids).*

4.20 *Hit the pavement. On your right is a municipal swimming pool.*

4.30 *The trail ends here (for now), next to the Raritan, east of Ironia Road. Return to Sunrise Lake.*

Patriots' Path North—Sunrise Lake to Historic Speedwell Village

0.00 *From the Sunrise Lake parking area, cross the Whippany River.*

0.10 *Bear right.*

> The trail that goes straight ahead here leads into an undeveloped section of the park that's open to bikes and worth exploring.

> *Go uphill, steeply at times, staying on the main trail. Other small trails will appear to your left.*

Along Patriots' Path

1.60 *From approximately 440 feet in elevation, the trail descends, bearing left. Watch for sparse square white markers. Pass through an open meadow.*

1.80 *Cross Whitehead Road, bearing left on the pavement and turning right after you cross the bridge.*

2.30 *Cross Washington Valley Road.*

3.00 Cross Sussex Avenue. The path is paved here (parking access).

3.40 Cross Inamere Road (parking access).

3.80 Cross Lake Valley Road (parking access).

4.00 At Lake Road, turn right, pass the recycling center, cross a bridge, travel uphill easily, and watch for the trail on your left.

4.50 Turn left onto the path.

5.10 Arrive at Speedwell Lake and the historic Speedwell Village. This landmark could use some serious cleaning up.

Turn around here and return to Sunrise Lake.

Information

Morris County Park Commission
PO Box 1295, Morristown, NJ 07962-1295
201-326-7600

Bicycle Repair Services

Marty's Reliable Cycle
173 Speedwell Avenue, Morristown, NJ
973-538-7773

Cycle Center of Denville, Inc.
Main Street and Route 46, Denville, NJ
973-627-2300

9

Allamuchy Mountain State Park—North Section

Location: *Morris, Warren, and Sussex Counties*
Distance: *Tour A, Jefferson Lake Loop, 4.1 miles; Tour B, Tranquility Farm Loop, 5.1 miles*
Terrain: *Hilly, rugged*
Surface: *Dirt, gravel, bedrock, loose stone, mud*
Maps: *Allamuchy State Park—North Section (inaccurate for trail use, fair for access point location); USGS Tranquility (not useful for trail navigation)*
Highlights: *Extended exploration on unmarked trails in a 5000-acre wild forest area; rail-trail miles available on the nearby Sussex Branch Trail; camping, picnicking, and trout fishing at Stephens State Park along the Musconetcong River; historic Waterloo Village*

While the Stephens section of Allamuchy Mountain State Park is highly managed, well marked, and well maintained, the north section is just the opposite—an amorphous blend of rugged hills; sandy and eroded trails; old jeep and fire roads; a long, rocky, central plateau; and a few large, oddly shaped blocks of intrusive private property. This unwieldy area, relegated to the park management's back burner, is either unmarked or so mismarked with a mixture of old paint blazes and tin scraps that blazed trail navigation is impossible. NORBA-sanctioned races are held here as well, and the temporary markers set up by the race committee add to the confusion. The maps in this book may be your best bet for navigation; the others currently available are inadequate.

This park is a strong and long-neglected contender for multiple-use development and enforcement (although it's arguably too rugged for snowmobile or equestrian use and is commonly abused by ATVs). It's accessible from the Sussex Branch Trail, which already sees off-road bike

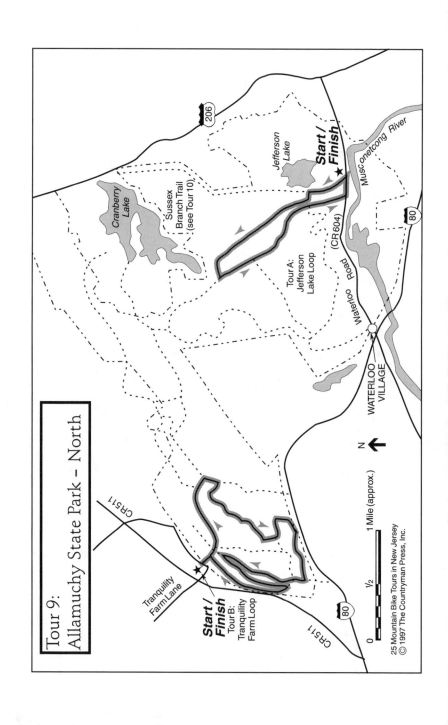

Tour 9:
Allamuchy State Park – North

Cranberry Lake

206

Sussex Branch Trail (see Tour 10)

Jefferson Lake

Start / Finish

Tour A: Jefferson Lake Loop

(CR 604)

Musconetcong River

80

Waterloo Road

WATERLOO VILLAGE

N

1 Mile (approx.)

CR511

CR511

Tranquility Farm Lane

Start / Finish
Tour B: Tranquility Farm Loop

80

0   ½

25 Mountain Bike Tours in New Jersey
© 1997 The Countryman Press, Inc.

use, and its development would pull aggressive cyclists away from Stephens and its more sensitive natural area.

Because the north section is rather large, it's easy to get lost in, and since it's a plateau, getting lost typically means a serious dose of hill climbs and descents to backtrack. The challenge of navigation in the north section has no doubt preserved the area's sense of remoteness and privacy—that and the fact that this is essentially very demanding terrain that ranks solidly in the expert class. An intermediate rider will walk a great deal, and beginners will be frenzied by the demanding climbs, log jumps, rocks, and erosion gullies that experienced riders easily manage and (profess to) relish. Still, within this stupefying trail system lies some amazing terrain, full of long, fast singletrack and dirt hills. The combination of terrain and open space may well rank this no-man's land firmly in the realm of the state's best mountain biking (from an advanced rider's perspective).

Tour A: Jefferson Lake Loop

The access point for this loop is off the Sussex Branch Trail (see Tour 10), a rail trail that begins on County Route 604, 0.7 mile east of historic Waterloo Village off I-80. If you're coming west on I-80, take exit 25, and then make a left at the second light onto US 206. Go 1.7 miles and you'll see the parking lot on your right.

If you're coming east on I-80, again get off at exit 25, and follow the signs for Waterloo Village. When you reach CR 604 (about 1.5 miles), the parking area is right in front of you across the road.

The parking area isn't well marked—it's just a large gravel lot with a sani-john and a currently blank signboard (welcome to Allamuchy North).

0.00   *Head north out of the parking area, following the rail trail.*

0.40   *Just as you come to Jefferson Lake, look to your left for a very small trail with white (paint) markers on the trees.*

It's easy to ride past this inconspicuous trail. If you see the blue paint blazes of the Long Path on your left, you've gone too far. Back up and look around.

Head uphill on the trail. This section is technical.

0.46 Turn right at a T.

0.47 Bear right at a Y. The right turn follows a flat section; the left goes uphill. The trail then climbs and becomes rocky and steep.

0.87 Cross an outcropping of exposed bedrock.

Some white paint is visible along this part of the trail. This is demanding and difficult uphill terrain, but the trail levels out shortly.

1.09 Crest out along the side of a densely wooded ridge.

1.26 Pass a large, conspicuous boulder on your right.

1.86 Go left at a T.

2.13 At a Y, bear left, climbing slightly.

2.40 The trail flattens and white markers appear sporadically.

2.54 Reach a Y and go left. Don't follow the white markers here, which bear off to your right.

2.93 Go left at a Y. The right-hand turn goes downhill and reconnects to your trail just ahead.

3.20 Cross a small, seasonal streambed and bear left at a Y. Go downhill.

3.90 The trail comes out onto County Route 604. Turn left.

4.10 Turn left into the parking area where you began.

Tour B: Tranquility Farm Loop

To reach the trailhead, get off I-80 at exit 19 and head north on CR 517. Go 1.4 miles, watching very carefully, and turn right onto a small, unmarked dirt road, directly across CR 517 from Tranquility Farm Lane. At 0.15 mile turn left at a T (to the right is a gated woods road) and park. A few hundred feet farther along the paved road, a road leads uphill to the right (east). Begin here.

0.00 Follow the dirt road uphill. The road curves to the left.

0.11 Turn right onto a trail where dirt has been piled to thwart the entry of off-road vehicles. There are some rusty old state park service signs here. Continue uphill.

0.20 Continue straight ahead, past a small concrete cistern on your left.

This cistern was created to hold water for a homestead downhill and to your left.

0.28 Pass a rocky, gullied trail on your right.

0.30 Pass another trail on your right.

All the trails in this area, including the one you're on, are heavily eroded and unmaintained. You'll encounter blowdowns, rocks, and mud in periods of runoff.

0.88 The trail begins to level out. Pass a trail to your left here.

0.97 Arrive at a T at the top of a rise and go right.

There's a wetland east of you, behind a thin buffer of hardwoods, which may not be visible during summer months. To your left is a small wooden footbridge.

1.08 Go right at a Y. Climb on a singletrack trail.

1.27 At this point the trail levels out somewhat, though terrain is rolling and rocky.

1.47 Begin to descend, crossing a series of small seasonal streams.

2.04 At a T, turn left and descend. The trail widens.

2.22 Bear right at the fence between the park and I-80. The trail soon goes uphill, following rocky, rolling terrain.

2.48 Merge with a wider trail and go right.

3.21 Pass a grove of mature white pines on your left and keep going.

3.27 Turn left onto a skinny singletrack at the end of the pine forest.

4.14 The trail hairpins to the right, heading toward County Route 517.

4.25 Pass a trail to your left.

4.26 Bear left at a Y.

4.36 *You come close to the road at this point, but bear right and stay on the trail, going around the steel gate and continuing on an old, broken-pavement surface.*

A long line of large sugar maples is on your left, a dense grove of their offspring on your right.

5.10 *Arrive at another steel gate. You'll recognize your starting point.*

Information

Stephens State Park
800 Willow Grove Street, Hackettstown, NJ 07840
908-852-3790

Bicycle Repair Services

Alpine Outdoors
207 Mountain Avenue, Hackettstown, NJ
908-852-0852

10

Allamuchy Mountain State Park— Stephens Section/Allamuchy Natural Area

Location: *Morris and Warren Counties*
Distance: *Blue-and-white loop (advanced intermediate), 5.24 miles; red-and-yellow loop (easier), 2.15 miles*
Terrain: *Hilly*
Surface: *Dirt, gravel, rocks, mud*
Maps: *Allamuchy Mountain and Stephens State Parks DEP map (free): Allamuchy Mountain State Park Stephens Section/Allamuchy Natural Area, DEP map (free)*
Highlights: *Gentle, intermediate-level trails in a quiet natural area; rail-trail miles available on the nearby Sussex Branch Trail; camping, picnicking, and trout fishing at Stephens State Park along the Musconetcong River; historic Waterloo Village*

The Allamuchy Natural Area is an attractive spot for low-key cyclists of any ability with an interest in exploration, nature, or easy riding through quiet woodlands. The area is used by hikers and equestrians but in general isn't well known. The use of this area by aggressive bikers seeking technical challenges is not recommended (expert riders should go to the north section of the park). The trails are narrow, their soils soft and sometimes muddy, but they are well marked and maintained. Several loop rides are possible here; I've described two. Families with able and experienced children have managed both, although there are some difficult sections that require walking.

To reach the Allamuchy Natural Area (also called the Deer Park or Deer Pond area), take I-80 to exit 19, and go south on County Route 517. At 2.2 miles, turn left onto Deer Park Road. (The official entrance

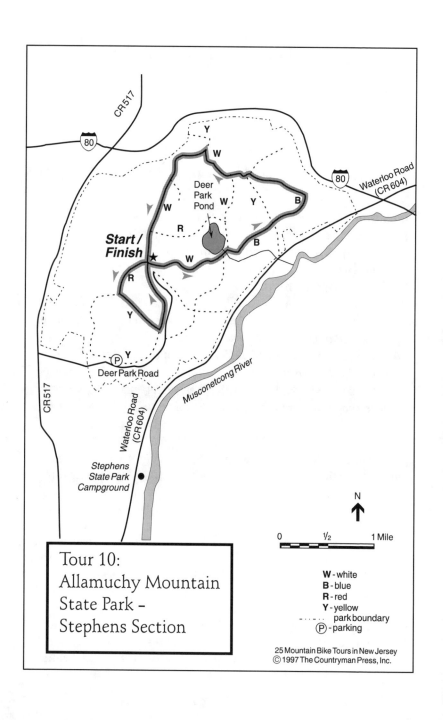

CR 517

I-80

Deer Park Pond

Y

W

W

W

Y

B

R

B

W

Start / Finish

★

R

Y

Waterloo Road
(CR 604)

I-80

R

Y

Ⓟ Y

Deer Park Road

CR 517

Waterloo Road
(CR 604)

Musconetcong River

Stephens
State Park
Campground ●

N

0   ½   1 Mile

Tour 10:
Allamuchy Mountain
State Park –
Stephens Section

W - white
B - blue
R - red
Y - yellow
······ park boundary
Ⓟ - parking

25 Mountain Bike Tours in New Jersey
© 1997 The Countryman Press, Inc.

to the state park is another 2.5 miles down CR 517 toward Hacketts-town. You can reach it by continuing south past Deer Park Road, turning left on Bilby Road, then left again on Waterloo Road.) Keep going on Deer Park Road until you reach a parking area at 0.7 mile. You may want to check the signboard here to see if any maps are available. Continue another 1.6 miles over a rough road, passing a private residence. Leave your car in the lot. If the gate is locked, you can park along the side of the road. Again, check the signboard box for maps, though almost all the trails are marked and self-guiding.

After seeing the condition of the dirt road, you may elect to park in the first lot at 0.7 mile and ride to the white and blue trailhead on your bike, following the road, which will add about 3.4 miles to your tour. If that's the case, you can cut out a section of road travel by following the yellow loop.

There are approximately 15 miles of trails in the Natural Area, so a good deal of exploring is possible outside the loops described here. If you're planning to spend the weekend at the Stephens State Park Campground, you can also ride your bike around there, as well as on a section of the Morris Canal towpath near Saxton Falls.

If the Natural Area proves too much for your group's abilities—which is unlikely—don't ignore the possibilities for riding on the Sussex Branch Trail, a 17-mile (round-trip), scenic, flat ride that will take you north all the way to the intersection of the 26-mile-long Paulinskill Valley Trail (see Tour 15). It follows the railbed of the Erie–Lackawanna Railroad, which operated between the mid-18th and 19th centuries. The old railbed crossed an earlier canal, built to carry coal and iron across New Jersey. Unfortunately, the canal itself and the towpath have been so interrupted by development that a long-distance bikeway along that route is not possible. It is possible to see a reenactment of the canal days, however, at nearby Waterloo Village, said to be an ancient meeting place and burial grounds of the Delaware tribe. Here you can see the beautifully preserved stone barns, a gristmill, a sawmill, shops, and mansions that evoke another time. Aside from the port itself (canal towns, particularly those with access to the Atlantic Ocean, sometimes accentuated their self-image and regional importance by referring to themselves as ports), the best part of the place is the 400-year-old Lenape village, complete with a costumed guide. You can't come in on your bike, though, and there's a fee.

The Blue-and-White Loop

0.00 *Ride around a gate to continue on the dirt road you came in on.*

This road curves around to the right, where a grove of large spruce trees gives way to a hardwood forest over dense fern cover. A pond appears through the trees on your left.

1.00 *Cross the bridge and dam at the spillway of Deer Park Pond. You're still on a road at this point. Watch to your right for the blue trail.*

1.10 *Turn right onto the blue trail here, which climbs slightly into the woods.*

Although the white trail officially heads straight and follows the lakeshore, white markers also appear on the blue trail. This is a skinny singletrack in most places that can require some technical skills. Blowdowns and rocks are frequent.

2.95 *Go straight at a T, where the white trail goes to the left (a shortcut back to the pond). Ignore any other trails you may see coming into the main trail here and there.*

This is heavily wooded and quiet forest.

The blue trail ends here. From this point, markers are white (and scant).

3.54 *Following an excellent singletrack trail, bear left at a Y.*

To your right through this section you will sense the presence of I-80. By turning right at this or the next intersection it's possible to reach a scenic area on the highway where there's a telephone, but the trail may be narrow and unmaintained. There are several other unmarked trails heading northerly as well.

3.78 *Pass a trail to the right.*

4.38 *Pass a trail to the left that climbs a small hill.*

4.83 *At a T, go straight.*

This is a junction with the red trail. It's not a four-way intersection, as shown on the DEP map. (Check out the one here.) A left would take you back to the white trail on the north end of Deer Park Pond. There are plenty of blackberry bushes here.

Deer Pond, Stephens State Park

5.18 *Go straight at a T. The well-marked red trail goes off to the right at this point, just before you get back to the road and your starting point.*

If you wish to add another 2.15 miles to your tour, follow the red-and-yellow loop directions from mile 0.06, turning right onto the red trail here.

Continue onto the road and turn right.

5.24 *Arrive back at the parking area.*

The Red-and-Yellow Loop

The red-and-yellow loop begins from the same parking area on Deer Park Road.

0.00 *Head through the gate as if you were continuing on Deer Park Road.*

0.06 *Turn left onto the red trail.*

This pretty, fast singletrack can be muddy.

0.74 *At a Y, go left on the yellow trail.*

This intersection is not well marked, although if you look around on the trees you'll eventually find some paint. Follow over rough, undulating terrain with roots, rocks, and blowdown.

1.45 *Arrive at Deer Park Road and turn left. Follow the road.*

2.15 *Arrive back at the parking area and your car.*

Several other trails remain to be explored. If you feel like adding mileage, try the rest of the red trail, which heads toward Allamuchy Pond, as well as the white trail around Deer Park Pond.

Information

Stephens State Park
800 Willow Grove Street, Hackettstown, NJ 07840
908-852-3790

Bicycle Repair Services

Alpine Outdoors
207 Mountain Avenue, Hackettstown, NJ
908-852-0852

11

High Bridge Line and Ken Lockwood Gorge

Location: *Hunterdon County*
Distance: *16 miles*
Terrain: *Flat, wooded*
Conditions: *Dirt railbed, dirt road, pavement*
Maps: *Hunterdon County Map; USGS High Bridge, Califon (for reference, but not necessary)*
Highlights: *Ken Lockwood Gorge Wildlife Management Area; fly-fishing-only section of the Raritan River; South Branch; historic towns of High Bridge and Califon; nearby camping at Voorhees State Park*

This is the flattest, prettiest ride in central New Jersey. Here you have the ideal tour for a lovers' retreat weekend (or a reconciliation, if it comes to that), an unforgettable family adventure complete with scary railroad bridges and storybook scenery along a rocky mountain magical river, a cycle-fishing ride along the most fabled section of the South Raritan's exclusive fly-fishing-only stretch, or a plain and simple exercise run between two charming, historic towns. All this in only 16 easy miles! Or less if you want. More scenic road miles are available, and there are other things to do along the way. Hybrids and mountain bikes are best for the terrain, but you could even handle this on a sturdy 10-speed.

With the native hospitality of the people of High Bridge and Califon and the pride they take having the trail connect their towns, this is the warmest, most inviting tour I've ever been on. There is something here—something almost palpable—that transcends the norm. Perhaps it's the strong sense of community. Perhaps it's this hallowed branch of river. And perhaps it's the fact that Califon, your destination, was the

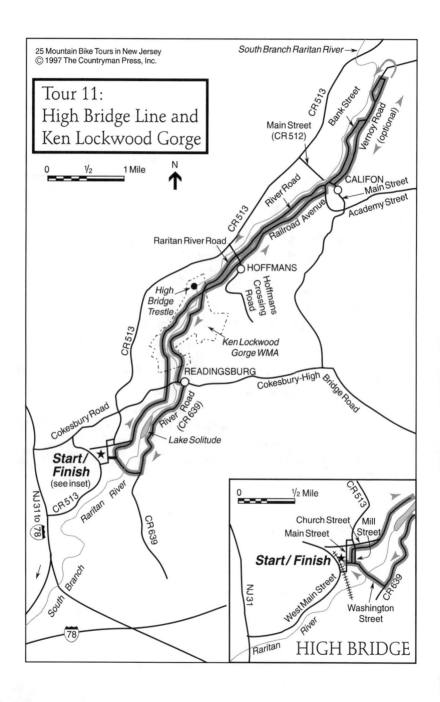

25 Mountain Bike Tours in New Jersey
© 1997 The Countryman Press, Inc.

Tour 11:
High Bridge Line and
Ken Lockwood Gorge

0   ½   1 Mile

N

South Branch Raritan River →

CR 513

Bank Street

Vernoy Road (optional)

Main Street (CR 512)

River Road

CR 513

Railroad Avenue

CALIFON
Main Street

Academy Street

Raritan River Road

HOFFMANS

Hoffmans Crossing Road

High Bridge Trestle

Ken Lockwood Gorge WMA

CR 513

READINGSBURG

Cokesbury-High Bridge Road

Cokesbury Road

River Road (CR 639)

Lake Solitude

Start/ Finish
(see inset)

CR 513

NJ 31 to 78

Raritan River

CR 639

South Branch

78

CR 639

0   ½ Mile

Church Street
Main Street

Mill Street

CR 513

Start/ Finish

NJ 31

West Main Street

Raritan River

Washington Street

CR 639

HIGH BRIDGE

first municipality in Hunterdon County to be placed on the National Register of Historic Places. You'll understand why when you get there.

The High Bridge Line itself—a historic, reconditioned railbed that you'll ride on for the first part of this tour—has been the focus of several county and state organizations, as well as a special project of the well-known New Jersey Rail Trails Association. This volunteer association coordinates and promotes rail-to-trail conversion efforts, and publishes both a newsletter and a series of maps dealing with the existing and in-progress rail trails across the state. High Bridge Line now contains some 16 unofficial miles. "Unofficial" means, in this case, that the right-of-way exists and is being developed, but that you can't necessarily ride it yet, because it's not officially open. Important things like bridges may be missing, and there may be obstacles such as forests and swamps, not to mention legalities like private property for which easements must be established. Undoubtedly, with the support that the linear trails in Morris and Hunterdon Counties are getting these days, there will be more rid-able miles very soon.

High Bridge, settled in 1700, is 2 miles north of NJ 31 at Clinton on County Route 513 north. It's just south of Voorhees State Park, which has a convenient family camping area (there's also camping at Round Valley and Spruce Run Recreation Areas, both nearby). After you go under the railroad bridge on West Main Street, turn left; you'll see the path on your right within a few hundred feet. Park where permitted. You'll see a Hunterdon County Parks System trailhead sign on the path. Plenty of parking is available on the expanded railbed itself, which also provides neighborhood parking.

If parking is a problem along Main Street, keep going north. A block after you turn right off Main Street as you follow CR 513 onto Church Street, turn right again on Mill Street. Within half a block the path crosses Mill Street, and there's plenty of parking on the right-of-way itself.

0.00 *Get yourself headed east, which will be easy since the rail trail doesn't go west from here. You're following a good dirt-and-gravel surface through a residential area.*

The path turns gradually to the northeast. Follow as it runs through the woods, next to and high above the Raritan River.

1.30 *Cross the Cokesbury Road Bridge.*

High Bridge Trestle over Ken Lockwood Gorge

You're still in a residential setting here, and may be wondering what happened to the river. The trail surface is excellent, and about what you would expect from a rail trail—only a bit more so. You can easily cruise about midrange on your middle chainring.

1.40 Now you see the river to your right, and the atmosphere turns rural.

Continue in this quiet and peaceful setting, with the river several hundred feet lower than the trail. There are some side trails around, if you feel like exploring, including one established-looking trail that heads down toward the river. As always, and especially in linear parks, observe postings.

2.80 *Cross High Bridge Trestle over Ken Lockwood Gorge.*

At the time of this writing, the bridge is not thoroughly planked. Though strong girts and a steel superstructure support it, it may be a less-than-encouraging prospect for some. There's no danger yet, but the bridge is deteriorating and has been the target of both vandals and arsonists. It's scheduled for repair in 1997—which may already be complete by the time you visit. Take some time to look up and down the gorge when you're on the bridge. This is a timeless spot.

3.50 *The river is now on your left. The trail continues northeast.*

3.80 *Cross Hoffmans Crossing Road.*

Take note of Raritan River Road, down the hill to your left. That's the road you'll be returning on, unless you opt to take the rail trail back to this point from Califon, and then get on the road.

4.40 *Cross a dirt road.*

Though the atmosphere becomes residential, the trail remains picturesque and wooded. The surface has changed to red clay here.

4.80 *Cross a private driveway.*

5.26 *Cross another private driveway.*

5.65 *Join Railroad Avenue in Califon.*

Califon Station, now a museum, is to your left. It's open on the first and third Sundays of each month, May through December. Built by the town's citizens at their own expense in 1870, it's now maintained by the historical society. According to local folklore, the town's original name, California (honoring a gold-rush baron who spawned the town with his wealth), was shortened to Califon because the citizen's couldn't fit California on the new train station's sign. Convinced?

91

Turn left and proceed into town on Academy Street.

Poke around. Note the quaint architecture, dating from Victorian and Revolutionary times. Pick up the flyer *Historic Califon,* only to discover similarities between it and my own text. See if you can find the grammatical error on the first page. Consider the self-guided tour of the *Homes, Businesses, and Their History,* using as a guide the flyer by that title. Such a tour—or even a perfunctory ride around—is, as the Califon Historical Society says, a "step back in time, a living example of a rapidly disappearing way of life—the small New Jersey town."

Now you have choices. You can return through Ken Lockwood Gorge, or you can go a little farther on the rail trail. If you haven't yet eaten lunch, there are a few more options to consider here, too. You can head back, stopping to eat in the gorge, right on the river's edge or on a boulder in midstream, in near total privacy (unless it's a weekend or a good hatch). You can eat on the wooden bench on the front porch of Rambo's (highly recommended, and you can't miss the place . . . just turn right onto Main Street and glance left). Take in the (generous) local color. You can head one block up to Bank Street and eat at the single picnic table at the rail trail, across from the Califon Fire Company. But if you're with kids, you'll almost certainly want to go 0.2 mile down Bank Street to Califon Island Park, where there's a fantasy wooden playground, a phone, and a bunch of picnic tables beside the river. The place is an island only by merit of a shallow, sometimes flooded ditch between it and Bank Street, so don't expect Key West.

Side Trip: Exploring Califon

If you want to add a few more miles, head down the trail opposite the fire company. You'll be able to mentally reconstruct its original layout on Academy Street from here, which is nearly in view.

0.00 *Follow the trail east. It parallels Vernoy Road and then joins it for a short distance.*

1.84 *The trail dead-ends as Vernoy Road sweeps around in front*

of it again. A trail sign here reads SOUTH BRANCH RESERVATION, HUNTERDON COUNTY PARK SYSTEM, COLUMBIA TRAIL, TEWKSBURY TWP. *The trail will continue past this spot in the future. Go left here, and follow Vernoy Road along the river and back past Califon Island Park, where it becomes Bank Street.*

3.55 *Turn right on Main Street and go to River Road, just before the bridge, which is in view.*

0.00 *Reset your odomotor. Go left on River Road, keeping the river to your right. You're on pavement.*

1.70 *Cross Hoffmans Crossing Road, which you'll remember from mile 3.8. Now you're on Raritan River Road proper.*

2.00 *The road turns to dirt and enters Ken Lockwood Gorge Wildlife Management Area.*

The river is approachable and languid in midsummer, yet large rapids are present in runoff periods. You'll see trout anglers here. It's possible to drive through the gorge, but the road is so poor that any cars you encounter are likely to be going slow. The place is actually very safe, and you can hear a car coming from way off. Still, watch those blind curves, especially if you have kids along. A plaque commemorating Ken Lockwood is set in a granite chunk just beyond the railroad bridge, on the left just before you get to the next bridge, a little stone arch. It was placed there by Trout Unlimited. Take your time and enjoy this ride; your actual distance in the gorge itself is short.

4.00 *The road becomes pavement.*

4.50 *Arrive at a major road. At this point the rail trail is to your right, within view a short way uphill on Cokesbury Road. Since there's no way to get on the trail except by climbing the steep trestle embankment, go left here on Cokesbury–High Bridge Road. (An access is planned for this bridge, so you may want to investigate.)*

4.55 *Turn immediately to the right onto River Road (County Route 639). This takes you along the river. The traffic isn't* bad and tends to be slow. Pass Lake Solitude, a widening of the Raritan River.

6.20 Bear right as River Road becomes Washington Avenue, passing a factory on your right.

6.35 Pass Union Forge Park on your left.

6.65 Pass McDonald Street on your left.

6.70 Turn right onto Mill Street and follow it uphill to your car (the street bears hard left after you turn onto it).

6. 85 Arrive at your car.

RIDGE AND VALLEY PROVINCE

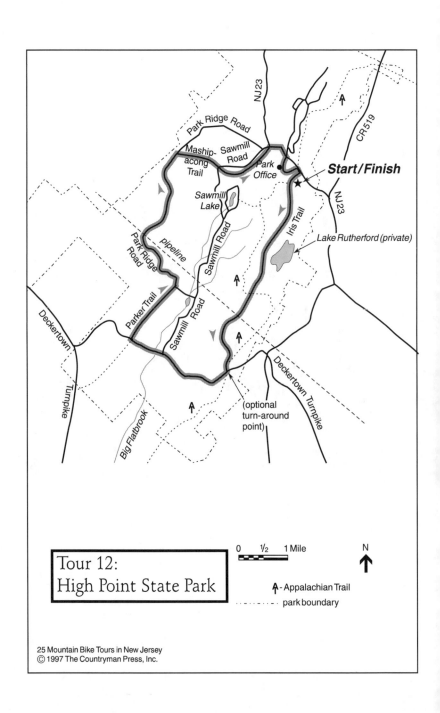

Start/Finish

Park Ridge Road

Maship-acong Trail

Sawmill Road

Park Office

Sawmill Lake

Park Ridge Road

pipeline

Sawmill Road

Parker Trail

Sawmill Road

Iris Trail

Lake Rutherford (private)

NJ 23

CR 519

NJ 23

Deckertown Turnpike

Deckertown Turnpike

Big Flatbrook

(optional turn-around point)

0   ½   1 Mile

N

Tour 12:
High Point State Park

⚑ - Appalachian Trail
········· - park boundary

25 Mountain Bike Tours in New Jersey
© 1997 The Countryman Press, Inc.

12
High Point State Park

Location: *Sussex County, township of Sussex*
Distance: *8.5-mile return trip or 13.4-mile loop with road miles*
Terrain: *Hilly (intermediate level and above)*
Surface: *Dirt—rocky, rooty, and sometime wet singletrack (return trip); paved and dirt roads with some singletrack (loop)*
Maps: *High Point State Park, State Park Service map (free)*
Highlights: *High Point Monument and scenic views; camping in tents and cabins; fishing, boating, swimming; Appalachian Trail access; proximity to Stokes State Forest, Delaware Water Gap National Recreation Area*

Located in the extreme northwest corner of the state, this park contains the highest ground in New Jersey. High Point itself offers panoramic views of three states, including the Catskill Mountains and Wallkill Valley to the north, the Pocono ridges to the west, and the farms and woodlands of Sussex County to the south and west along the edges of the prominent Kittatinny Ridge. Hikers as far away as the southern Catskills and the Shawangunk Ridge (where you'll find the best mountain biking in New York, by the way) can see the monument on High Point (1803 feet), and it has served as a landmark for aviators, hikers, bikers, and anyone else navigating through this scenic section of the tristate area. The monument is a war memorial to the state's soldiers, designed in the likeness of the Bunker Hill monument—though the obelisk actually looks like a scaled-down version of the Washington Monument.

The park itself has long been a popular destination for hikers, primarily because a section of Appalachian Trail runs through it—from just north of Sunrise Mountain to the south on up to the New York State line. (The AT then takes a peculiar turn to the southeast, forced to remain in New Jersey until it finally makes the crossing from Abram S. Hewitt State Park.) Within High Point Park itself are 14 miles of trails. Considerable attention has been paid to them in hiking guides, and several are open to mountain bikers and equestrians; the latter seem to use the trails more than the former.

There's plenty to do here besides bike, if you have a weekend outing in mind. Aside from the extensive woodlands (at 14,000 acres, this park is huge), there's tent and cabin camping, swimming, boating, fishing, access for disabled people, and an 800-acre natural area featuring a cedar swamp with rhododendron undergrowth that's populated with birds of a wide-ranging and unexpected variety, from the least bittern to the great crested flycatcher, not to mention the yellow-billed cuckoo (and didn't you think the cuckoo was extinct?). Although they have been sighted in the park, you're not likely to see bobcats, southern bog lemmings, or the elusive Florida packrat.

You may, however, spot that oddly peripatetic creature known as the Appalachian Trail end-to-ender. These reclusive and threadbare critters have been known to slog nearly 2000 miles just for the fun of it and can be recognized by their worn boots, their happy-yet-hangdog expressions, and their tendency to ask, "How far's Maine?" Though sightings are rare, the number of people end-to-ending is said to be increasing. You're almost certain to see the lesser weekend wannabes, though, or the section-at-a-timers who can't schedule in a full migratory experience. You'll recognize all of them by their patched packs, dented Sierra Club cups, and faded bandannas swabbed in fly dope. Give all ATers plenty of room as they file past you because you do have to cross their trail once or twice, which is a sort of honor.

The only restrictions to mountain bikes at High Point are the trails in the natural area and, of course, the AT itself. While the Monument Trail is legal at this time, I don't recommend it—it's hard on your tires (and if there are ever user conflicts in this park, I'll bet they start here). Do visit High Point, however. You can pedal up the Scenic Drive or go up in your car.

The park can be reached easily from New York or Pennsylvania by taking I-84 to exit 15 in Port Jervis and traveling south on NJ 23 about 4.5 miles to the park office. Coming from the north, the park office will be on your right. From the southeastern part of New Jersey, it's convenient to take NJ 23 north until you reach the park, about 7 miles north of Sussex. Trail maps, overnight parking permits, and historic information as well as an excellent display of indigenous Native American artifacts are available at the park office.

Park at the AT parking lot, which is just south of the park headquarters on NJ 23 (and just before the park's maintenance headquarters). The AT access trail goes into the woods here. You're not on the AT proper, so don't worry. The park people want you to park here. Your destination is trail #10 on the green park map, known as the Iris Trail.

0.00 *Enter the woods at the trailhead.*

0.20 *Turn left onto the Iris Trail. Trail markings vary from red paint to white rectangles with red dots in the middle.*

1.50 *Continue on.*

Around here you'll begin to get views of Lake Rutherford (private). You may also see the stumps of American chestnut trees, which were logged off after the 1920s chestnut blight. Although the blight destroyed most of the eastern forest chestnuts, there are still a few small trees to be seen.

2.23 *Pass a trail to your right.*

2.30 *Bear right at the edge of private property. A trail goes to your left.*

3.30 *Cross the Tennesco Gas pipeline and continue straight.*

The trail narrows and becomes rockier.

4.09 *Following an ascent, you'll see the AT cross your trail.*

4.25 *The trail ends at two large rocks just before you reach Deckertown Turnpike.*

To your right 0.5 mile, at the AT parking lot, there is a water pump.

At this point you can turn back on the Iris Trail. If you don't mind combining peaceful road miles with sections of the Parker and Mashipacong Trails, which will mean going about 4.9 miles farther than you would by turning around here, go right on the turnpike for the 13.4-mile loop.

Taking the loop allows you to ride most of the legal trail miles in the park. *Note:* The Parker Trail is highly technical.

4.75 Pass the AT parking area on your right. (There's water here.)

5.80 Pass Sawmill Road on your right.

6.30 Watch carefully for the Parker Trail, marked with light blue paint blazes, which crosses the road here. Turn right (north).

Parker Trail is generally well marked but very rocky in places. It connects High Point State Park to Stokes State Forest to the south.

7.50 Turn left onto Park Ridge Road, a very quiet and scenic park road.

10.50 Turn right onto the Mashipacong Trail, blazed in yellow paint.

The trail is just across Park Ridge Road from the entrance to the Natural Lands Trust Reinhardt Preserve.

11.50 Cross Sawmill Road.

12.20 Cross the old road to Sawmill Lake.

12.80 Arrive at a three-way intersection with Park Ridge Road and NJ 23 in a cabin and campsite area. Turn right onto NJ 23 and ride the shoulder back to the park office.

You can find shortcuts back to the office from here if you search around, and you can avoid NJ 23 from the park office to the AT parking lot by portaging your bike through the woods in the southwest corner of the office property.

13.40 Arrive at the AT parking lot.

Information

High Point State Park
1480 State Route 23, Sussex, NJ 07461-3605
973-875-4800

Bicycle Repair Services

Coyote Bike and Ski
9 Main Street, Sparta, NJ
973-729-8993

13
Stokes State Forest

Location: *Sussex County, Town of Branchville*
Distance: *17.25-mile loop, optional miles available*
Terrain: *Rolling hills, steep ascents (advanced intermediate)*
Surface: *Rocks, mud, flats, dirt, singletrack and limited pavement*
Maps: *Stokes State Forest State Park Service Map (free), NYNJTC North Kittatinny Trails #17 and #18. For trail list and descriptions request NJ Department of Environmental Protection and Energy publication* Stokes State Forest Trail System
Highlights: *Full camping facilities; fishing, swimming, day use, boating; proximity to Delaware Water Gap National Recreation Area, High Point State Forest, Tillman Ravine Natural Area*

This particular part of the country is well suited to the off-road/on-road touring cyclist, if there ever was or is such a thing. Here's my vision: the ability to tour the country by hybrid or all-terrain bicycle, taking only trails and scenic back roads, carrying an ultralight outfit (tent, pad, and sleeping bag), touring by day, and camping or even riding by night. In the future, as bottomland rail trails and canal corridors increase in number and length, connecting scenic mountainous regions and state parks, such a sport may become more practical—and popular. The key to enjoying it would be the careful combination of lightweight climbing and backpacking equipment, bombproof panniers and accessory packs, and a lightweight, suspended bicycle of appropriate design. *Bikepacking.* Think about it: The romantic appeal of backpacking is added to mechanized, distance-devouring bike touring. Freedom from the inevitably busy roads touring cyclists get stuck on. Camping for free in the state parks and forests. The key is to go light. Nothing superfluous. No luxuries other than an engrossing paperback.

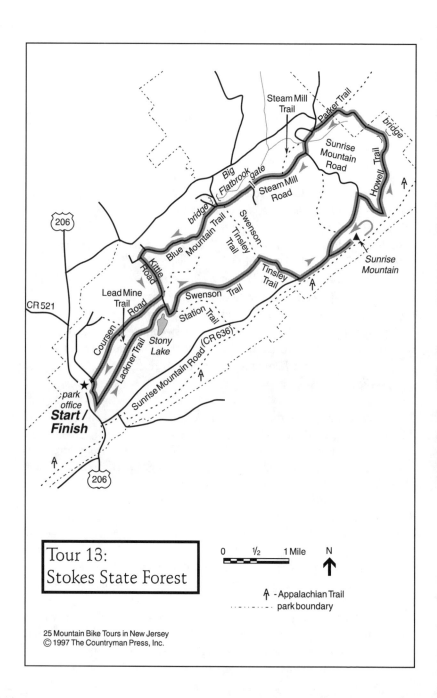

Steam Mill
Trail

Parker Trail

bridge

Sunrise
Mountain
Road

Big
Flatbrook
gate

bridge

Steam Mill
Road

Howell
Trail

206

Blue Mountain Trail

Swenson-
Tinsley
Trail

Little
Road

Sunrise
Mountain

Lead Mine
Trail

Tinsley
Trail

Tinsley
Trail

CR 521

Coursen

Swenson   Trail

Lackner Trail

Station Trail

Stony
Lake

Sunrise Mountain Road (CR 636)

park
office
**Start /
Finish**

206

Tour 13:
Stokes State Forest

0   ½   1 Mile   N

⋏ - Appalachian Trail
········· park boundary

25 Mountain Bike Tours in New Jersey
© 1997 The Countryman Press, Inc.

Stokes State Forest is located between High Point State Park to the north and the Delaware Water Gap National Recreation Area to the south and west. All three are connected by dirt roads and trails and have designated bike routes and tent or cabin camping areas. Trails and scenic rides on quiet roads are abundant—too many to experience even in several days of aggressive exploration. There are 24 hiking trails in Stokes State Forest alone on which mountain biking is permitted, in addition to several rough roads classified "four-wheel-drive accessible" (Shay, Cross, Dimon, and Woods Roads). The combination of deep forest, clear streams, and Kittatinny Ridge's jagged heights makes the Stokes trail system for any purpose attractive enough; the fact that the trails legal to off-road cyclists are technically challenging hills as well as easy lowland flats amounting to some 20 miles of riding makes it one of the most biker-friendly parks in the state. Don't hesitate; just go.

The main entrance to the forest is off US 206, roughly 10 miles south of Milford, Pennsylvania. It's about 15 miles south of Port Jervis (I-84) off County Route 521 (which is also US 206). Look for the entrance on the left. You've gone too far if you hit CR 636 (Sunrise Mountain Road).

Enter the park office lot. You can leave your car here. Go inside and ask for a map and any updated information regarding mountain biking. They have maps, information, bathrooms, and an old-tool display, as well as a few mastodon bones the CCC dug up in the park. This is a comprehensive day-use and camping area with a variety of facilities for picnicking, partying, camping, boating, swimming, and softball.

0.00 *Head into the park past the main entrance on Coursen Road and look to your right.*

0.10 *Turn right and go through a gate onto a dirt road. This is the Lackner Trail.*

0.35 *Watch carefully to your left for the trail. Turn left as the trail leaves the dirt road and follow it across a very small concrete dam.*

The trail continues, flat and wide, through an oak, hickory, birch, maple forest.

1.35 *The Lead Mine Trail will appear on your left. (It's not on the park map.) Go straight.*

In case you need to know, the Lead Mine Trail goes out to

Coursen Road over generally level terrain, according to the trail system pamphlet.

1.90 *You'll see the western end of Stony Lake on your right through the trees.*

2.10 *The Lackner Trail joins Kittle Road. Turn right.*

2.45 *Arrive at the Stony Lake picnic and beach area. There are bathrooms, picnic tables, and a swimming area. Near the signboard in the parking area, locate the Station Trail. Travel uphill on this trail.*

2.60 *Turn left onto the Swenson Trail, with red markings.*

This junction is not shown on the park map—it's covered by the P that designates the parking area. Check out the one in this book.

4.50 *At a T where the Swenson Trail joins the yellow Tinsley Trail, turn right and go uphill.*

The park map incorrectly shows a four-way intersection here. The Swenson Trail actually continues to the left on the Tinsley Trail, in case you want to ride it in the future.

5.20 *At Sunrise Mountain Road (paved), turn left. This road is one way, in your direction.*

Soon you'll pass a scenic overlook. You can see pieces of the Southern Catskills from here, including Table and Peekamoose Mountains.

Continue on.

5.25 *Take a right here and climb if you want to see the summit of Sunrise Mountain.*

6.30 *You'll have to dismount and hike a short distance to the view east. (There are rest rooms here.) Return to the main road.*

7.10 *Turn right onto Sunrise Mountain Road, where you came up the hill.*

8.60 *Turn right onto the Howell Trail.*

This trail is well defined. The surface is grassy and, in spots, heavily gullied. The middle of the trail acts as a seasonal streambed. You're going uphill.

8.60 *Turn left with the Howell Trail. Just ahead and uphill a little way is the Appalachian Trail.*

The introduction to Tour 12 has more information on the AT.

9.05 *Bear left at a Y, watching for gray markers. The trail is rocky.*

9.70 *Bear left at another Y, immediately crossing a wooden bridge.*

9.90 *At yet another Y, bear left again. Marking is very poor here.*

10.60 *Join the Parker Trail. Turn left.*

At this point you are actually in High Point State Park (see Tour 12 for details on connecting the two parks). This section of the Parker Trail is flat and fast.

11.10 *Turn left onto Sunrise Mountain Road. Pass Steam Mill Campsite. Just across the bridge south of the campsite loop, with a wetland on your left, pass a small trail on the right. This is the Steam Mill Trail. Don't take it. Continue.*

11.20 *Turn right onto Steam Mill Road (abandoned). Go easily downhill until you reach a gate.*

12.30 *At a Y, where a gated road begins, go straight.*

12.80 *Pass the Swenson–Tinsley Trail on your left.*

13.10 *Turn left before the bridge into the Ocquittunk Camping Area.*

13.05 *Immediately, look left by the first campsite and follow the Blue Mountain Trail, which begins just across the brook.*

This is a long, rocky, excellent trail.

14.40 *At a T, go left, pass through a tumbledown stone wall within a hundred feet or so.*

14.50 *Hit pavement. This is Kittle Road. Head left, passing some barns. Cross a creek and bridge (built in 1960) and go uphill.*

15.25 *Arrive at Kittle Field Recreation Area.*

There are bathrooms and tons of picnic tables here, as well as a feeder creek of Big Flatbrook, which is said to contain trout. It's dirt dry in August.

Go to the intersection of Coursen Road, which runs along the southern perimeter of Kittle Field, and turn right (or, if you're diehard, keep going straight and pick up the Lackner Trail and turn right, retracing your earlier steps).

17.25 Arrive back at the main entrance parking area.

Information

Stokes State Forest
1 Coursen Road, Branchville, NJ 07826
973-948-3820

Bicycle Repair Services

Coyote Bike and Ski
9 Main Street, Sparta, NJ
973-729-8993

Delaware Water Gap
National Recreation Area

You'd think that finding a decent ride in a natural area of 72,000 acres (in this case a National Park Service Recreation Area) would have been easy, right? After all, there are excellent tours available in some New Jersey parks of less than 1000 acres. But it wasn't. In the Kittatinny Point Visitor Center I overheard a representative tell a hopeful inquirer, "No, there are no trails for mountain biking here." Already decked out in her Lycra body suit, the biker turned and left, obviously as surprised and disappointed as I was. *Seventy-two thousand acres and not a single bike trail?*

A tremendous number of recreational pursuits go on in the Gap. Hikers, joggers, and backpackers jam the trailheads to Mount Tammany, traverse the Appalachian Trail from Dunnfield to Walpack in increasing numbers, and have their own sanctioned parking areas bedecked with those enviable and user-friendly HIKERS ONLY signs. Touring cyclists cruise the immensely popular Old Mine Road from Montague to Kittatiny Point demanding—by inference, tradition, and sheer numbers—the right-of-way over the few touring motorists; noisy flotillas of resounding aluminum canoes come down from launch sites as far north as Hancock, New York; Boy Scout troops, youth and tour groups, buses full of schoolchildren, strollers, campers, boaters, tubers, picnickers, photographers, birders, hunters, anglers, equestrians, rock climbers, and sightseers of every description fill and enjoy this incredible resource (it is still peaceful; in places, serene). *But where are the bike trails?* The National Park's publication *Spanning the Gap* explains: "Attention Bicyclists: Bicycles are not allowed on any *trail* within Delaware Water Gap National Recreation Area. You are allowed to use all paved and unpaved, ungated roads in the park." So the answer becomes soberingly apparent: *There aren't any.*

There are two good reasons for this. The first is simply that mountain bikers are the most recent user group on the scene, and proactive members are just lifting the lid for a peek inside. The second is that, as a branch of the federal government, the National Park Service is a hard nut to crack. It is by nature more demanding than the average municipality when it comes to formal trail designation. There are impact studies and park-regulations amendments to be considered, and that means more red tape. Many miles of trails are suitable for mountain bikes in the vast Water Gap, but none are dedicated yet.

This will change soon. The area's management is not philosophically opposed to mountain biking. In fact, some managers are enthused about it, and the park service maintains a continuing relationship with the Kittatinny Mountain Biking Association (KIMBA), organized by Lyle Lange of Mountain Sports in 1994. Lange, IMBA northwestern New Jersey regional representative, has been working on issues of trail access and designation in the Water Gap since 1991 with New Jersey District Ranger Barry Sullivan and his staff.

In anticipation of their first mountain biking trail system, park officials have conducted costly environmental impact studies in the Blue Mountain Lakes area and were working with KIMBA at the time of this writing to develop a trail maintenance and protection program for the 13-mile system. Just as other municipalities in the state of New Jersey are looking for assurances that trail guardianship is conducted and promoted by its respective user group, the National Park Service wants the same thing. To meet the park service's expectations, KIMBA is organizing at this time (and looking for members, by the way). The trail is expected to open in the summer of 1997.

In the meantime, however, National Park Service policy states that unless a trail is designated specifically for bike use, bikes are not allowed on it. The only exceptions are those dirt roads open to public vehicular traffic. It's not permissible to ride the fire access roads or park maintenance roads (which are used by official park service vehicles for maintenance).

But don't give up on the Delaware Water Gap; it still has great places to bike. Aside from the roads described in these tours, there are many more, paved and dirt, on both the New Jersey and Pennsylvania sides of the Delaware River. This is the kind of place that's worth visiting for its own sake, regardless of your recreational preference.

Still, even if it's dirt and hills and obstacles—the heart of technical riding—that you want, you've come to that special place between heaven and earth: The Delaware Water Gap is joined at the hip with Stokes State Forest to the northeast, which is the singletrack capital of western New Jersey, bar none. If it makes you happy, think of this area as one huge, 100,000-acre landmass with two different sets of rules, two different topographies, and the same general location.

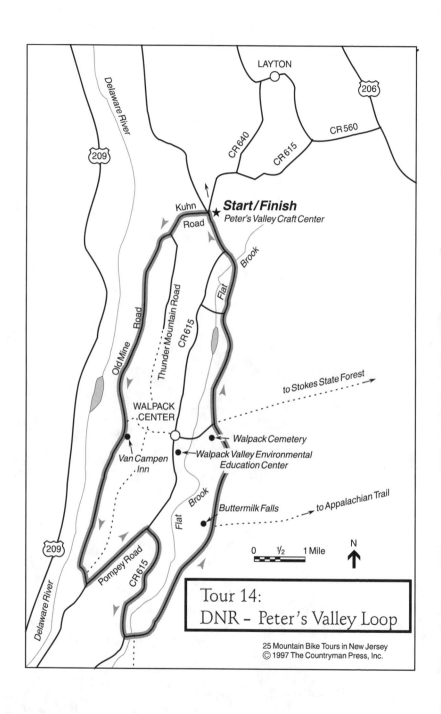

LAYTON

206

Delaware River

209

CR 640

CR 615

CR 560

Kuhn
Road

Start/Finish
Peter's Valley Craft Center

Brook

Flat

Old Mine Road

Thunder Mountain Road

CR 615

to Stokes State Forest

WALPACK
CENTER

Walpack Cemetery

Van Campen
Inn

Walpack Valley Environmental
Education Center

Flat Brook

Buttermilk Falls

to Appalachian Trail

209

Pompey Road
CR 615

0   ½   1 Mile

N

Delaware River

Tour 14:
DNR – Peter's Valley Loop

25 Mountain Bike Tours in New Jersey
© 1997 The Countryman Press, Inc.

14

Delaware Water Gap National Recreation Area—Peter's Valley Loop

Location: *Sussex County*
Distance: *15 miles*
Terrain: *Gently rolling hills, flats*
Surface: *Dirt, gravel, pavement*
Maps: *Delaware Water Gap Official Map and Guide, National Park Service, NYNJTC, North Kittatinny Trails, map #17, Sussex County map*
Highlights: *Peter's Valley Craft Center; Delaware River scenery; Flat Brook; Buttermilk Falls; nearby Millbrook Village; Worthington State Forest, historic sites, park visitors centers*

As you investigate the biking opportunities in the Delaware Water Gap, the first thing people will tell you, raising their eyebrows as if they have a secret, is how beautiful the place is. (With 4 million visitors annually, far below the anticipated 10 million, the area is considered by many to be a well-kept secret.) Then they'll mention the Old Mine Road. If they really know the area, they'll say, "Have you ridden the dirt roads around Walpack? If you haven't . . . you don't know what you're missing."

This is undeniable. Even if you resist road touring, take the opportunity to see this large central section of the Water Gap, which many people feel is its most attractive piece. This tour focuses more on the scenery and culture than on the ride itself. There is no technical terrain. (Maybe a few hills.) And, although the surface is mostly dirt, there are some sections of paved road to travel, which—depending on the day of the week and the time of year—may require experience and caution. This is a ride for the touring mountain biker who wants a break from

Along the Delaware

the pounding terrain available at nearby Stokes State Forest (see Tour 13) and a place that's suitable for an extended day outing. Here, along the Delaware River and Flat Brook, there are numerous romantic spots in which to photograph, lunch, or nuzzy up.

Delaware Water Gap National Recreation Area is easily accessible from both New York and Philadelphia. It's between I-84 to the north and I-80 to the south; accessible off US 209 to the west (first you have to cross the Delaware River) and US 206 to the east.

A good place to begin this forest and river tour is from the Peter's Valley Craft Center (between Layton and Walpack Center on County Route 615), where you can see traditional and contemporary crafts in a quasi-historic setting, if you're into that kind of thing. There's a pricey, upscale outlet store and gallery here, open April through December. Village studio artists welcome the public in July and August; both locals and out-of-towners work in a variety of media from blacksmithing to pottery to wood, textiles, and photography.

You'll probably be more interested in the Water Gap's other rural (and infinitely more organic) historic village of Millbrook (1832), however, which is a re-created 19th-century "living history" community staffed by unpaid volunteers. The thing to catch, especially with your kids—or your lover—is the Millbrook Days celebration, a harvest-style festival held every fall during which the entire village is on display. The "locals" dress in period fashions and demonstrate a wide variety of domestic, agricultural, construction, and homesteading skills and trades from colonial times forward. It's a spectacle ranking firmly beyond quaint, similar in quality to Mystic Seaport or Sturbridge Village but on a scaled-down, less pretentious, earthier and more hands-on level. Millbrook isn't open every day, but you can always walk through it. You might find the general store open, though. Call ahead, and plan to visit when you can, or you'll have missed the most romantic spot in the Water Gap.

It's possible to take this tour with younger children, but you'd probably be wise to cut out the road miles on its north and south ends, and instead of making a loop tour, stick to the dirt roads. (Go south to Buttermilk Falls from mile 14.40, or south along the Delaware River and back, from mile 0.8, to avoid all the pavement and most of the vehicular traffic. Traffic is slow and light on these dirt roads.)

Find a place to park in Peter's Valley Craft Center and get yourself heading west on Kuhn Road: From the intersection in the village, this is the road to your right if you came south from County Route 640, and on your left if you came north on CR 615.

0.00 Head west on Kuhn Road, climbing uphill. This short section of road is paved.

0.50 Pass a wetland area to your left.

0.70 Pass Thunder Mountain Road on your left.

0.80 At a T, go left onto Old Mine Road.

0.95 The road turns to dirt and descends slightly.

1.60 The Delaware River appears on your right intermittently, interrupted by fields and forests.

2.65 Pass the Van Campen Inn on your left.

This two-story stone inn was built around 1746 and immaculately restored by the National Park Service. It's open only on Sundays from May 19 through October 20, 1–5 PM (call 973-729-7392).

3.05 The river reappears.

4.35 Bearing left (south), away from the river, you'll cross a small one-lane bridge.

4.45 Turn left onto Pompey Road.

This is a paved road with bumpy, broken shoulders that's open to public traffic, even though current versions of NYNJTC map #17 may show it as "Authorized Vehicles Only" (authorized park roads are off-limits to cyclists). Travel uphill.

5.65 At the T, go right on CR 615 south.

Be careful: This is a very scenic area, but you'll have to concentrate a little on the traffic, which can be heavy on weekends. The shoulder here is poor to nonexistent, but there is room to bail out if you must. Weekend drivers are used to cyclists in the Gap and are generally very biker-friendly. Watch for renegades.

Climb. There's an expansive view of the Kittatinny Mountains and valley to the northeast.

7.15 After a residence, turn left off CR 615 and onto an unnamed dirt road that goes slightly downhill.

7.35 Turn left, and go over the bridge at Flat Brook. Continue straight, though you'll see a dirt road to your right that departs for the backcountry toward Donkey Corners.

This is a trail that would be suitable for mountain biking—an old truck or fire road that would require no trail construction, minimal marking, and a circuit possibility using Hamilton Ridge Road and Millbrook Village as a focal point.

9.85 *Arrive at the impressive, cascading Buttermilk Falls, a popular scenic destination.*

The blue Buttermilk Falls Trail (strictly a hiking path) departs this point to access, within a mile or so, the 2100-mile-long Appalachian Trail. The AT is our country's first National Scenic Trail, extending from Georgia to Maine along the Appalachian Mountain Range; 70 miles of it is in New Jersey. The AT, too, is strictly a hiking trail.

Continue straight ahead.

11.85 *On your left is Walpack Cemetery and the road to Walpack Center.*

This historic hamlet is now the location of the Walpack Valley Environmental Education Center, a National Park Service/ Eatontown Board of Education cosponsored facility. The program takes one class of students at a time and is open to all schools and environmental organizations. A side trip to the center will require a 1-mile round-trip detour from this point, but there's not much to see that you can't see from County Route 615. To your right at this point, a seasonal road enters Stokes State Forest, passing through Tillman Ravine.

12.25 *Pass a few residences and a sign that says* ROAD NOT MAINTAINED.

13.45 *Pass a road on your left, which heads out to CR 615.*

14.10 *Go left at a Y. Cross a few small bridges over the upper realms of Flat Brook. This is the Flatbrook-Roy Wildlife Management Area. Continue until you merge with CR 615.*

14.40 *Turn right to merge with CR 615. Follow the road to Peter's Valley.*

15.00 *Arrive in Peter's Valley.*

Information

Delaware Water Gap National Recreation Area
Bushkill, PA 18324-9999

Dingmans Falls Visitor Center
717-828-7802
Open May 11 through September 15, Saturday and Sunday 9–5

Kittatinny Point Visitor Center
908-496-4458
Open May 10 through October 20, daily 9–5;
during the winter season, Saturday and Sunday 9–4:30

Peters Valley Craft Center
19 Kuhn Road, Layton, NJ 07851-9702

Millbrook Village
908-841-9531

Worthington State Forest
908-841-9575

Bicycle Repair Services

Coyote Bike and Ski
9 Main Street, Sparta, NJ
973-729-8993

15

Paulinskill Valley Trail

Location: Sussex and Warren Counties
Distance: Stillwater to Sparta Junction: 26.58 miles round trip;
Stillwater to Brugler Road: 28.14 miles round trip
Terrain: Flat
Surface: Gravel, cinder, dirt
Maps: This trail is self-guiding. A serviceable map is now available from
Kittatinny Valley State Park. Some county maps also show both current and discontinued railroad rights-of-way.
Highlights: Extended riding through a diverse area of farmlands, woods, and abandoned fields; camping, swimming, boating, and mountain biking trails at nearby Swartswood State Park

This is one of the longest, flattest off-road rides in the state. Imagine, a place to ride your bike for over 50 miles round trip, unimpeded, without traffic, with (almost) all bridges intact, and with a state park that has a beach and camping near the trail's midsection. The Paulinskill Valley Trail doesn't have technical dirt or singletrack, and it sure doesn't have hills, but if you just want to relax and ride, or have an off-day workout or idyllic family tour without having to focus on trail surface for a change, this is the place to come. These are peaceful and picturesque rail-trail miles. Along the way you'll share the path with browsing deer, flocks of turkeys, consistent views of the Paulinskill—which you ride next to for miles—and the subtle, old-time scenery and feeling of the towns, horse farms, and valley of the Paulinskill's headlands. You'll also pass through quite a few small hamlets and crossings where you can stop to rest and look around.

You can access this trail almost anywhere there's a road crossing and travel as far as you like, but the most attractive place to begin, and to see

Stopping along the Paulinskill

the whole trail in two easy trips, is at the trail's midpoint: Water Wheel Farm, on Cedar Ridge Road in Stillwater. By beginning here, you have a choice between two tours: east to Sparta Junction and back (26.6 miles round trip) or west to Brugler Road in Knowlton (28.14 miles round trip). These distances are within the reach of most active bikers, and more aggressive riders may attempt to do them both at once, for a total of 54.75 miles.

The trail began with a 1970s grassroots effort by a group of people who formally came together in 1984 as the Paulinskill Valley Trail Committee. Their involvement led to the purchase of the right-of-way with Green Acres acquisitions funds, money generated from bond issues. The New York, Susquehanna & Western had abandoned the track in 1963, which was a summer of serious drought. Anticipating possible future water shortages, the city of Newark bought the line in order to run an aqueduct from the Delaware River to the Newark Watershed (also known as the Pequannock Watershed), a 35,000-acre system of five major reservoirs in Passaic County. The city retains the right to build the aqueduct. If it does, cyclists will someday be riding over a subterranean pipeline, but not much else will have changed.

From NJ 94, about 6 miles south of its junction with US 206 in Newton, turn right—or north—onto Fairview Hill Road (from points along these roads you'll see some of the finest views in New Jersey). At 0.9 mile turn right onto Fredon–Marksboro Road, then left in 0.1 mile onto Dixon Road. At this quaint crossroads, you'll be on a parcel of Water Wheel Farm (you can see the operating waterwheel from this point). However, the trail starts down at the bottom of Dixon Road, where it becomes Cedar Ridge Road, another 0.5 mile ahead and near the farm's horse barns. There you'll see the Paulinskill Valley Trail sign. You can park on the left.

The right-of-way you'll be riding on is approximately 66 feet wide, and the entire corridor is enclosed by private property. In some cases the trail passes through private backyards. Be careful to stay on the trail. You may encounter horses, but vehicles are not permitted on any part of the trail. The Paulinskill Valley Trail is now managed by Kittatinny Valley State Park.

East to Sparta Junction

0.00 Head east, keeping Water Wheel Farm to your right. The trail is obvious.

0.58 Wall Street.

0.93 Stillwater Station Road.

1.56 County Route 610.

2.36 Kohlbocker Road.

2.72 CR 614.

5.08 CR 622.

6.03 Plotts Road.

7.93 Downer Road.

8.10 CR 519 (Old Halsey Road).

9.18 US 206.

9.81 NJ 94.

10.93 Bridge #4.

11.01 CR 663.

11.05 Intersect with the Sussex Branch Trail (Warbasse Junction).

This rail trail is another bike route with considerable promise, although at this time there are obstacles and surfaces are not ideal. However, it's worth exploring if you have the time. By turning right here (southwest), you can go about 14 miles to Mt. Olive. If you go left, within 1 mile you'll enter Lafayette, a small town with several antiques stores. The Sussex Branch Trail follows the old bed of the Erie–Lackawanna Railroad, which carried ore, freight, passengers, and agricultural products from the mid-19th to the mid-20th centuries.

Continue heading east. The trail turns south slightly.

11.63 Bridge #3.

11.67 Garrison Road.

12.45 CR 623.

12.46 Bridge #2.

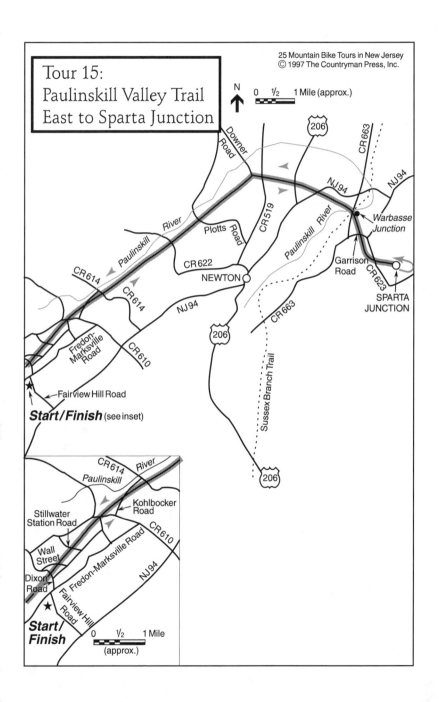

Tour 15:
Paulinskill Valley Trail
East to Sparta Junction

25 Mountain Bike Tours in New Jersey
© 1997 The Countryman Press, Inc.

N

0   ½   1 Mile (approx.)

Downer Road

206

CR 663

NJ 94

NJ 94

Paulinskill River

Plotts Road

CR 519

Paulinskill River

Warbasse Junction

Garrison Road

CR 614

CR 614

NEWTON

NJ 94

CR 622

CR 663

CR 623

SPARTA JUNCTION

206

Fredon-Marksville Road

CR 610

Fairview Hill Road

Sussex Branch Trail

206

Start/Finish (see inset)

CR 614

River

Paulinskill

Kohlbocker Road

Stillwater Station Road

CR 610

Wall Street

Fredon-Marksville Road

NJ 94

Dixon Road

Fairview Hill Road

★

Start/ Finish

0   ½   1 Mile

(approx.)

12.93 Bridge #1.

13.29 Sparta Junction, eastern terminus. The trail ends here. Turn around.

West to Brugler Road

0.00 *Facing west, with a farm pond on your right, follow right along the edge of the pond on the rail trail.*

1.34 Henfoot Road.

1.76 Stillwater Road.

2.83 Bridge #5.

3.54 Spring Valley Road.

4.74 Bridge #6.

5.36 Bridge #7.

5.79 East Crisman Road.

5.94 Bridge #8.

6.48 NJ 94.

6.69 Arrive at Footbridge Park.

Welcome to Blairstown. This is a good place to get off the trail for lunch. Take a right in the middle of the park, cross the footbridge, and you're there. The haphazard collection of stores and gas stations on NJ 94 is not a fair representation of Blairstown. To see the old section of town—which is just on the north side of NJ 94—follow CR 602 for a few hundred yards, and watch to your left. Quaint streets, historic buildings, and the lands of Blair Academy converge here.

Continue southwest on the rail trail.

8.65 Lambert Road.

9.83 Gwinnup Road.

10.28 CR 655.

11.33 West Crisman Road.

11.65 Bridge #9.

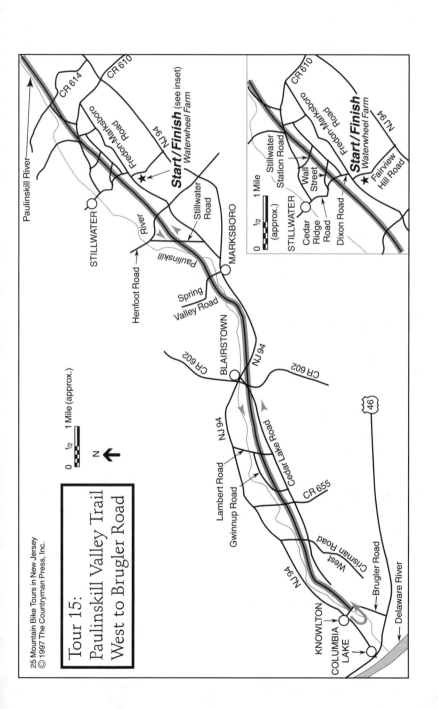

25 Mountain Bike Tours in New Jersey
© 1997 The Countryman Press, Inc.

Tour 15:
Paulinskill Valley Trail
West to Brugler Road

N

0   ½   1 Mile (approx.)

Paulinskill River

CR 614

CR 610

Fredon-Marksboro Road

NJ 94

STILLWATER

Henfoot Road

Paulinskill River

River

Start/Finish (see inset)
Waterwheel Farm

Stillwater Road

MARKSBORO

Spring Valley Road

CR 602

BLAIRSTOWN

NJ 94

CR 602

NJ 94

Lambert Road

Gwinnup Road

Cedar Lake Road

CR 655

West Crisman Road

Brugler Road

NJ 94

KNOWLTON

COLUMBIA LAKE

Delaware River

46

0   ½   1 Mile (approx.)

Stillwater Station Road

CR 610

Fredon-Marksboro Road

NJ 94

STILLWATER

Cedar Ridge Road

Wall Street

Dixon Road

Start/Finish
Waterwheel Farm

Fairview Hill Road

12.63 Station Road.

12.90 Erie–Lackawana Viaduct.

14.07 Arrive at Brugler Road.

This is the official end of the trail, according to the original Paulinskill Valley Rail Trail right-of-way survey from 1987. Mileages are taken directly from the survey to assure uniformity and to reduce the potential for confusion, but these figures may be adjusted in the future.

The railbed actually continues from here until it dead-ends on US 46 south of Columbia Lake. It is possible to follow the trail, and the surface is good, although marking and maintenance are poor, primarily because these are private parcels that you need permission to cross. Turn around here, and return to your starting point.

Information and Maps

Swartswood State Park
PO Box 123, Swartswood, NJ 07877-0123
201-383-5230

Kittatiny Valley State Park
PO Box 621, Andover, NJ 07821-0621
201-786-6445

Bicycle Repair

Coyote Bike and Ski
9 Main Street, Sparta, NJ
201-729-8993

The Bike Shop, Ames Plaza
Route 206, 17 Hamptonhouse Road, Newton, NJ
201-579-5310

PIEDMONT PROVINCE

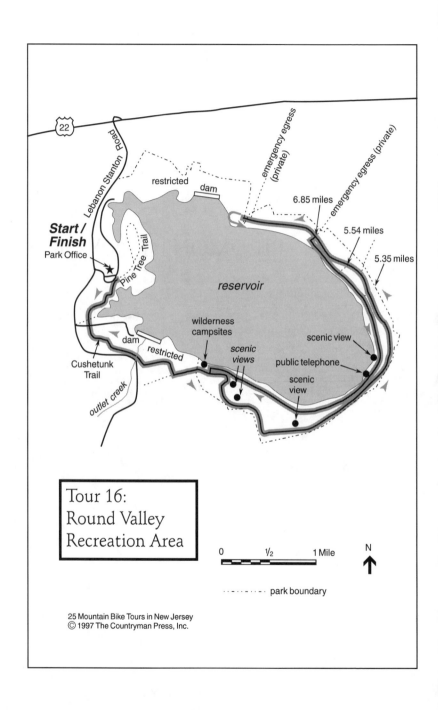

Tour 16:
Round Valley
Recreation Area

0   ½   1 Mile

N

·········· park boundary

25 Mountain Bike Tours in New Jersey
© 1997 The Countryman Press, Inc.

16
Round Valley Recreation Area

Location: *Township of Clinton, Hunterdon County*
Distance: *16.1 miles*
Terrain: *Rocky, hilly, expert trails*
Surface: *Dirt, gravel, cinder, rocks, logs*
Maps: *Round Valley Recreation Area, Division of Parks and Forestry, State Park Service (available at gate, see text for comments), USGS Califon, Flemington (helpful, but trail not shown)*
Highlights: *Swimming, fishing and boating, scuba and skin diving; wilderness camping; picnic areas; access for people with disabilities*

My heart sank as I drove south on County Route 513, from High Bridge toward Round Valley. I had inquired at a local shop about the trail at Round Valley, and a suspiciously sedentary-looking person told me, "The trail is hilly, rocky, and . . . terrible." Still, I hoped for the best.

The first people I met at Round Valley were a lively unisex crew of hard-core mountain bikers wearing team jerseys and riding suspended bikes. In their brilliant colors they circled the Wilderness Parking Area deftly, cooling down from a 20-mile ride. All wore helmets and a satisfying coat of sweaty dust. For a trail researcher, these are *the* people to meet. When I asked them about the trail, they all responded with elated jargon: "Awesome!" "Best place to ride in New Jersey!" "Kick butt!" "Slammin'!" "Tremendous singletrack!" "Lots of hills, but . . . boulders the size of your head!" So far, so good. I discovered that they'd never ridden nearby Allamuchy North (very similar terrain) or any of the northern parks. These riders described themselves as "fallen angels" from the Watchung and South Mountain Reservations—closures that hit them hard, they said—forcing them to travel far. As they rode off, leaving me to self-consciously ponder my helmet size, another guy, nursing a greasy chainring gash on the back of his calf, cheerfully asked if I needed help. It turned out he was the most knowledgeable, most local rider in the group. I was getting the coveted "emissary" treatment. He sized me up. After nearly a thousand miles researching New Jersey's trails over the past year, I knew I looked anything but green, unless it was with envy.

"You're gonna love this," he said with a grin. "Take two tubes if you have them." (I had only one tube and about 15 patches. It would have to do.) "Nice bike . . . how do you like it?" As I nodded, he studied the unified rear triangle of my Y bike. "That dual suspension will come in handy here. Anyway," he added as he rode off, "I always seem to break something or lose something on this trail. Take it easy on the downhills your first time. It's really fast and sudden. And watch out for horses."

Many people use this park, and fewer of them will be mountain bikers if we, as a group, don't respect the resource and help to maintain it. There's already some friction, as this park does indeed absorb pressure from nearby areas that have closed their doors to bikes.

I can't add much more in the way of sound preparatory advice for riding in this rugged and challenging terrain, except to say that water is available in several places at the Wilderness Campsite (check the regulations on using the Wilderness Area road first; if permission is denied, you must stay on the trail) and the pocket maps the park hands out are inadequate for navigating the bike trail. The trail itself is self-guiding, but you'll need to know where to exit in the event of injury. This book's map places park egresses in an approximate position (they're easy to find on the trail). *Please note:* These exits cross private lands and are to be used only in an emergency; they may be fenced off by the time you read this. There's also a phone at the Wilderness Camping Area, about midride. Since this park is a narrow strip of land between the reservoir and private property, it's difficult to get lost.

Still, the shopkeeper I spoke with was partially right. This *is* a "terrible" trail—for beginners and families with young or inexperienced children. It's an expert trail, and nobody should go alone.

Enter the Round Valley Recreation Area from I-78 at the Lebanon exit. The entrance is about 1.7 miles south off US 22 on Lebanon Stanton Road. Come through the main gate and take the first right into the Wilderness Camping Area parking lot. The Cushetunk (bike) Trail begins here, slightly uphill from the lot in a stand of pine trees. It's marked with yellow dots and distinctive green-footprint signs about the size of a real shoe. There's a signboard in the lot to orient you, complete with IMBA rules. You may encounter hikers and horses throughout the tour. Yield to both. The sign says you're about to cross a mountain range. This is true. Be prepared.

0.00 *Keeping the reservoir to your left, head east on the dirt singletrack.*

This is an incredibly scenic spot. Since the turns are tight and narrow in dense brush, beware of hikers. (Ordinarily they don't venture much beyond the first few scenic areas; most go to the nearby Pine Tree Trail, where you aren't permitted to bike.)

1.10 *Cross a pavement access road that leads to a dam. This area is restricted. Pick up the trail directly on the other side of the road. Go uphill into woods.*

1.20 *Pass a private home on your right, then descend steeply alongside a chain-link fence.*

1.75 *Come into an open area with the high earthen dam uphill and to your left and Lebanon Stanton Road on your right. Cross the paved access road and the outlet creek, and push up a very steep, short hill on the opposite side.*

The trail is well worn. Beware of an established ground nest of white-faced hornets midway up the hill, right in the middle of the trail where you're most likely to trash yourself (a few of them generously escorted me away from the nest).

1.90 *Along here the trail levels and the fence ends.*

2.20 *Now in deeply wooded surroundings, cross a gravel path that says NO BICYCLES in both directions. Proceed straight ahead, then bear left, climbing.*

2.45 *Reach a T at the top of a hill. There's a pavilion through the woods on your left, slightly downhill, and a vague path to your right that leads to a residential area. Horse trail markers and a red arrow point to the left here. Go left.*

2.50 *The trail bends to the right, passing a PRIVATE PROPERTY, NO BIKES sign on the left, then goes gently uphill through a maturing oak forest.*

2.70 At a T, go left and slightly downhill.

3.00 Enter the trailhead of the Wilderness Campsite, at a four-way intersection marked with a large sign and rules list. The campsite trail is a wide gravel path, which you can ride on your return trip if it's permitted (again, check the latest park regulations). Turn right here, climbing.

3.25 The trail turns hard right here at a Y, switching back, continuing uphill.

The trail that goes straight ahead is well used but dead-ends in about 25 feet at a rock slide that was never cleared. Because there are no trail signs at this point, people continue to follow to the dead end, only to turn around again.

3.50 At a T, go left and uphill. A skinny trail to the right goes downhill. Your trail climbs.

3.70 The trail is now leveling out, high above the reservoir to your left in a hardwood forest. Continue, level to downhill on some exceptional, fast singletrack.

4.37 At a T, go left. Two little trails merge here.

This may be some of the best singletrack you've ever seen. Be careful; you may run across a few broken bike parts and some teed-off horses (unlike mountain bikers, beasts of burden don't profess to love hills).

5.35 You're now at the bottom of the hill you just came down, standing at a Y. To your left, the dirt singletrack trail drops downhill.

This is the recommended route for equestrians, since it gets rockier ahead. (There's water down that way. Just go right at the bottom of the hill at 5.8 miles and find a pump at 5.9. There are more opportunities for water ahead.)

To your right, the trail continues a few hundred feet to a point where you can see a private home ahead of you. Proceed in that direction (right), and immediately look very, very carefully to your left for the trail. Don't go as far as the house or the posted signs.

Marking for the trail you want is currently nonexistent except for a vague sliver of surveyor's tape, which is easy to miss. As a general rule, the trail follows the flat top of the ridge through a rock garden, then onto more great singletrack. Look for trail wear and chainring marks on logs. You'll find it.

5.37 *Bear left and proceed along undulating flats on the ridgetop; begin to descend.*

5.54 *Go straight, past a singletrack on your left. This trail goes down to the reservoir.*

5.62 *Cross a gravel path.*

6.29 *Go straight, past another singletrack on your left to the reservoir.*

6.85 *Reach a four-way intersection. Go straight. The left trail goes to the reservoir, the right goes uphill and out of the park (use for emergency egress only).*

For the next 1.5 miles you'll encounter the most technical trail of this trip, due to the rocks and logs in the trailbed. If you don't wish to take it you can turn left here, go down to the gravel reservoir path, turn left, and follow the tour directions backward from the Wilderness Camping area intersection (see milepoints 3.00 and 13.10 for orientation).

8.20 *At a T, the trail goes left and dead-ends at the reservoir in 0.08 mile. To the right, the trail climbs very steeply and leaves the park over private property. Turn around here, or go left and take a break beside the reservoir.*

9.52 *Back at the four-way intersection (the 6.85-mile point), turn right and go downhill to the reservoir. If you've got the OK to enter the Wilderness Campsite, proceed with the following directions. If not, return the way you came by going straight at this point.*

9.60 *Turn left, following the gravel path that runs through the Wilderness Campsite (with its bathrooms and water pumps).*

10.80 *Continue on.*

There's a public telephone on your right.

131

11.00 This is a scenic spot, where a gravel shore area looks out over the reservoir. Continue following the gravel path.

13.10 Arrive at the Wilderness Campsite signboard (same as mile-point 3.00). Turn left here after regaining the trail you came in on, and follow it back to your car. (The gravel path continues straight but soon reaches private, restricted property. You can't get back to the parking lot on this trail, unfortunately.)

16.10 Arrive at the Wilderness Camping Area parking lot and your car.

Information

Round Valley Recreation Area
908-236-6355
Fees: Fee from Memorial to Labor Day except on Tuesday.
Hours: Call or inquire at gate. Parking areas open to 7:30 PM, varying seasonally. Tickets given.

Delaware and Raritan State Park

Besides, I want to tell you, there were pretty good times and many a heartbroken and rough life on the canal.
—Laura Henry, locktender

I don't know of an off-road ride as scenic, charming, and historically rich as the Delaware and Raritan Canal path. Nowhere else in the state will you find villages so varied and picturesque, waterways so clean and accessible yet visually wild, or riding surfaces so well maintained, marked, and manageable. Amid wood and iron-strapped gates against rock-sided locks, beneath shadows of stout, lamplighted inns, deeply textured with hand-laid stone and timber, all coiffed in the gentle curve of the green towpath berm, you'll feel that you've discovered something very significant; you may even sense the remnant pride in the tragic struggle for freedom here along Washington's Delaware. From the spires of Princeton along the wooded river's edge to the rocky bluffs of Upper Black Eddy you will travel, spellbound—in the near-audible footsteps of another time.

The D&R is a linear park, or simply a greenbelt some 64 miles long (one way) and perhaps only a few hundred feet wide, containing 3600 elongated acres. It actually consists of two canals: the Main Canal, which runs 33.90 miles from New Brunswick to Trenton, and the Feeder, which follows the Delaware from Trenton to Frenchtown, a distance of 29.96 miles. Both have towpaths. The Main Canal's ditch itself was originally 7 feet deep and 75 feet wide, while the Feeder was 6 feet by 50 feet; both generally maintain these dimensions today. Between the river and canal is the narrow, elevated riding surface, a doubletrack wide and surrounded by woods.

The project was conceived in the 17th century by William Penn as a means of joining New York to Philadelphia by water across the narrowest section of the state. Nothing was done for a hundred years, however, until the question of independence was resolved. When the canal was finally completed in June 1834, oceangoing vessels on the Raritan River could swap cargoes with canal boats in New Brunswick and trade directly with towns along the Delaware, although most of the commerce was in eastbound coal shipments. In fact, the D&R's maximum annual shipping (3 million tons, 80 percent coal in 1871) surpassed that of the Erie Canal's. This trip, which took about 2 canal days, previously required a 2-week ocean detour around Cape May. The industrial age was upon us, and the canalway quickly engendered a prosperous regional economy.

Each canal path is a total round trip of nearly 70 miles—difficult, though not impossible, to bike in a single day. However, their extremes (especially those of the Main Canal) are in urban or transitional zones, some of which are interrupted by road detours or can qualify as "demographically challenged." I've thus described the two most serene and attractive day outings possible. They should allow you time to relax and smell the roses.

17

The Delaware and Raritan Canal: The Feeder Canal—Washington Crossing State Park to Bull's Island

Location: Mercer County, Hunterdon County, and (in Pennsylvania) Bucks County

Distance: 26.9 miles, with shorter/longer loops possible

Terrain: Flat, wooded

Surface: Gravel, crushed stone, dirt

Maps: D&R Canal State Park (highly recommended free pocket map); standard Mercer, Hunterdon, and Bucks County maps; USGS Lambertville, Stockton, Lumberville (for reference but not necessary)

Highlights: Extensive river and canalside touring through 18th- and 19th-century townships; possibilities for hiking, canoeing, and camping; Bull's Island Recreation Area; Washington Crossing State Park in New Jersey and Washington Crossing Historic Park Memorial Building and Visitor Center in Pennsylvania; sightseeing in New Hope, Pennsylvania; assorted historical attractions

Gear up for a heavy dose of chic, chivalry, and charm. From the classy shops and quaint streets of New Hope to the solemn monuments and colonial landmarks of Washington's Crossing; past the locks, aqueducts, stately inns, and magnificent river scenery of the lower Delaware Valley; this is a ride that bridges contemporary and historical America by means of a rural, off-road bicycle path.

It's said that purists contest the status of the Feeder as a true canal, since it was designed simply to provide water for the Main Canal. Nevertheless, it looks just like a canal should, and it fits colloquial definitions, which run the gamut from ditch to groove, gully to trench.

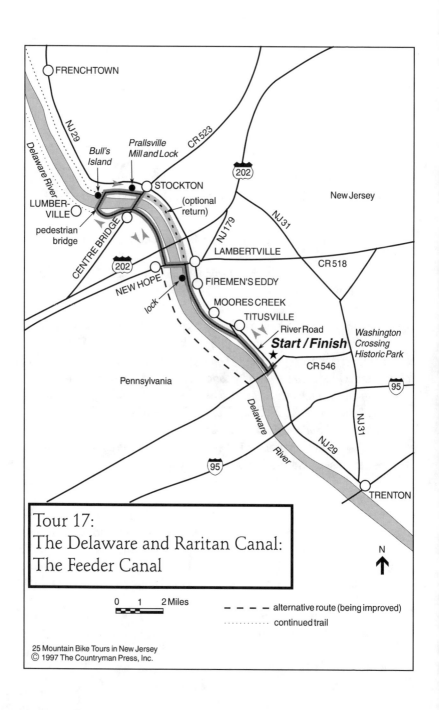

FRENCHTOWN

NJ 29

Delaware River

Bull's Island

Prallsville Mill and Lock

CR 523

202

STOCKTON

(optional return)

New Jersey

LUMBER-VILLE

pedestrian bridge

CENTRE BRIDGE

202

NEW HOPE

lock

NJ 179

NJ 31

LAMBERTVILLE

CR 518

FIREMEN'S EDDY

MOORES CREEK

TITUSVILLE

River Road

Washington Crossing Historic Park

Start / Finish

★

CR 546

95

Pennsylvania

Delaware River

NJ 31

NJ 29

95

TRENTON

N

Tour 17:
The Delaware and Raritan Canal:
The Feeder Canal

0   1   2 Miles

— — — alternative route (being improved)

· · · · · · · · · · · continued trail

25 Mountain Bike Tours in New Jersey
© 1997 The Countryman Press, Inc.

From its origin it also had barges, a towpath, and the requisite, balking beasts of burden. Later—by 1843—steam-powered boats relieved the grateful mules. The berm also shared a railroad bed. Call it what you like, this tour next to the Feeder Canal could very well be the best "non-canal" ride in the country.

Much of this has to do with the museum quality of the canals themselves. (There are actually two: one on the New Jersey side of the Delaware, another on the Pennsylvania; you get to ride both.) Most of the D&R canal system and many of its structures are still intact and are entered into the National Register of Historic Places. The Pennsylvania canal, the linear Delaware Canal State Park, is said to be the only remaining "continuously intact remnant of the great towpath canal-building era of the early and mid-19th century" (and nobody to date has contested this side's status as a true canal, so its self-esteem is high).

Like the Main Canal, the Feeder has daunting potential for extended outings. If you add the Feeder's mileage to the 60 (approximate) miles of Pennsylvania's Delaware Canal, there's a total of some 90 off-road miles, one way. As even Thomas Jefferson might have conceded, however, not all miles are created equal. The towpath in some parts of Pennsylvania can be ragged and slow in comparison to the smooth-riding D&H's, and in many places, the scenery isn't there. Urban transition zones compromise the aesthetics of the southern reaches of both paths (Trenton, New Jersey, and Tullytown, Pennsylvania), while the northern extremes are neither as popular nor as established as the well-traveled central sections on both sides of the Delaware River.

Connecting these venerable middle miles are several bridges, placed frequently enough to allow you to modify the tour I've described without having to backtrack. Still, this tour is designed to give you a comprehensive sampling of the area's attractions—spots that would be a shame to miss—while riding the most accommodating trail surfaces. Of course, as a day tour it has limitations; you may want to explore the rest of the trail at another time. And if 25 miles is your idea of pushing it for a casual day outing (you can always just turn around), consider an overnight along the trail at one of the many bed and breakfasts or at the haunting Bull's Island Campground. This would enable you, next day, to explore winsome Frenchtown or even the woodsy hinterlands of Upper Black Eddy (lauded by many as the nicest part of the Delaware Valley), Durham Furnace, and north into Easton, a diamond-in-the-rough coal town on the Pocono fringe where you can watch migratory fish leaping the ladder into the Lehigh River. You get the picture: Flower sniffers might take a lifetime to ride both paths; hammerheads can do it in a day or two. Whichever category you fall into—most of us overlap considerably—you'll agree that this is a most gratifying ride through uncommonly attractive territory.

The tour begins in Washington Crossing, just north of Trenton off NJ 29. From I-95 in Trenton, go 2.5 miles north on NJ 29 to its intersection with CR 546. Turn left as if you were going to cross the bridge. Immediately after your turn, look north along the river's edge and go right into Washington Crossing State Park. You can park anywhere.

0.00 *Head north out of the parking lot, keeping the river to your left. Don't bother getting on the towpath yet, which is to your right between the parking area and NJ 29. At the north end of the park, follow straight onto River Road. Go through the little hamlet of Titusville, with river views to your left. This area is included in the nationally registered Historic District.*

1.85 *Turn left onto the canal path as River Road joins NJ 29. Head north on the flat gravel surface.*

Watch for pedestrians, joggers, and so on. No horses are allowed on the Feeder Canal. There are fields and woods through this section.

3.40 *Pass Moores Creek access.*

4.50 *Cross a small bridge.*

5.40 *Pass Firemen's Eddy.*

The trail consists of long straight runs and wide, sweeping curves.

6.00 *To your left is a V-dam and, across the river, a large condominium complex in a reconditioned mill.*

6.49 *At this point a dirt path on the left leads down to the river.*

6.60 *Arrive at Lambertville Lock.*

7.00 *Enter Lambertville.*

Lambertville has an outstanding collection of Victorian buildings, and "nearly the entire city," to quote the master plan, "comprised of about 1800 structures, is on the State and National Registers of Historic Places"! Here there are two locks, two aqueducts, lock- and bridgetender's houses, a stone culvert, and several other canal ruins and remains. Paper, rubber, saw-, and flour mills were powered by water diverted from the canal. Development plans for the Lambertville section call for canal boat rides through town, for the restoration of canal facilities, and for the reconstruction of the outlet lock so that ferry service to New Hope can be restored.

At this time the trail through Lambertville is incomplete, locked in a right-of-way dispute. It's a relatively simple matter to divert: Turn left on Coryell Street, continue north unimpeded to Frenchtown by crossing the canal and turning north again, and follow the tracks under the power line and the US 202 bridge. But you can think about that later.

7.20 *Turn left onto Bridge Street (NJ 179) and walk your bike across the Delaware to New Hope, Pennsylvania.*

This is a short, friendly bridge with good views of the valley north and south of you.

7.40 *Arrive in New Hope.*

Have a look around. There's a good deal to see in this thriving colony of the arts: boutiques and music stores, jewelry and antiques shops, and especially restaurants, which will make you sorry you brought your lunch. Console yourself in regard to the fineries: The best things in life are still free.

Here you need to decide whether to continue north on the New Jersey side (see above) or on the Pennsylvania side of the river. These directions take you along the Pennsylvania side.

The canal path begins again off NJ 179 south, just up the hill from the bridge you crossed over on. As you're coming up this hill, while still in sight of the bridge and just before you hit the railroad tracks, turn right through a parking lot and you're there. Head north, with the river to your right, the canal to your left. You're on your way to Centre Bridge. Pass beneath a number of little bridges and a big one (US 202).

10.40 *Arrive in Centre Bridge.*

Stopping along the Raritan River

13.90 *In Lumberville, just before you reach Lock 12 (which is worth going the couple of hundred feet out of your way to look at), you'll see the pedestrian bridge to Bull's Island as you pass the Black Bass Inn. North of Lumberville on the Pennsylvania side the path continues, but the surface degenerates into a single strip of dirt or grass. It's not as companionable, as fast, or as easy as the New Jersey path. Cross the river to the recreation area.*

14.00 *Arrive at Bull's Island Campground.*

While camped here alone on Halloween Eve, I carved a pumpkin and fed the pulp to a friendly but strangely animated and ravenous group of 50 feral geese. In the dark, empty campsite—my jack-o'-lantern smirking ghoulishly—I imagined that these birds were the souls of Irish immigrant canal workers, scores of whom I knew had died of Asiatic cholera and were buried in unmarked, mass graves somewhere on Bull's Island. Beneath my very feet, perhaps.

On the welcome dawn I inquired at the ranger's office about the birds. "Immensely popular and the most photographed geese alive," I was told by Ranger Barbara Leon. It seems that from its origins as just one abandoned pair, the flock had grown to the point that management perceived them as a nuisance and moved for extirpation. A squabble ensued, which spawned the creation of the "Joint State Commission to Protect the River Geese" (seriously). Even some Pennsylvania legislators were involved (in the fight). And the geese remained.

Go and say hello, maybe offer the birds your lunch from New Hope. Take a quick ride around the campsite and you should spot them—or vice versa.

But beware the Natural Area! It seems that some parks people were digging a privy hole when they came upon a rather large bone. Obviously, it was a leg bone, but nobody could tell from what. So they sent it to Rutgers University. The good folks at Bull's Island (almost certainly a misnomer) were relieved to hear that the leg bone was a mule's.

Leave the campsite by continuing straight off the bridge toward NJ 29.

To the north, just under 10 miles away, is Frenchtown. The path surface is excellent all the way, and it continues with diminished quality to Milford.

14.10 Turn right when you see the path, heading south toward Stockton.

17.20 Arrive at Prallsville Mill and Lock.

This noteworthy and unusual site contains nine buildings from as early as 1796. Many community events are held here. There's a lock and several canal "races," with interpretive signage. Take a look.

Head south.

17.50 Arrive in Stockton, another attractive town on the river's edge. To avoid the (minimal) detour in Lambertville, turn right onto Bridge Street, which will take you back over the river to Centre Bridge. Continue south.

19.90 Pass under the bridge at US 202, and continue on the railroad right-of-way, crossing a small wooden bridge into town.

Cross the canal at Bridge Street and turn right onto the canal towpath, heading south.

Retrace your earlier route back to Washington Crossing Historic Park. But instead of turning right onto River Road, where you originally entered the trail, keep going straight.

26.90 *You'll see the park on your right.*

Information

Feeder Canal Office and Campground
Bulls Island Recreation Area,
2185 Daniel Bray Highway, Stockton, NJ
609-397-2949

Delaware Canal State Park,
11 Lodi Hill Road, Upper Black Eddy, PA
610-982-5560

Washington Crossing Historic Park
215-493-4076

Bicycle Repair Services

Freeman's Bicycle Shop
52 Bridge Street, Frenchtown, NJ
908-996-7712

18

The Delaware and Raritan Canal: The Main Canal

Location: *Mercer and Somerset Counties*
Distance: *25.3 miles round trip, with additional miles available*
Terrain: *Flat, wooded*
Conditions: *Gravel, dirt*
Maps: *D&R Canal State Park (highly recommended free pocket map); standard Mercer and Somerset county maps (Mercer maps often contain Princeton University inset); USGS Princeton, Hightstown, Rocky Hill, Monmouth Junction, Bound Brook (for reference but not necessary)*
Highlights: *Extensive river and canalside touring through 18th- and 19th-century townships; short tour of Princeton University and Township; possibilities for hiking, canoeing, camping; Princeton Battlefield State Park*

There are many ways to approach a return-trip ride on the Main Canal, but, unlike the Feeder Canal, there are no possibilities for a loop on this path unless you do road miles. The tour I've described begins and ends at Princeton, combining the best of the path's urban and rural environments. A mini-tour of the town itself at the end of your ride lets you explore its university, bookstores, restaurants, shops, museums, and historic sites. Group members who may not want to bike the entire distance can easily spend hours afoot here.

Weekend use of the Main Canal is very high, if not at "carrying capacity," so if possible plan your trip for a weekday. Arrive early and park at the Alexander Road access. (Parking at other access points can be a problem, although there are plans to improve the situation.) There's

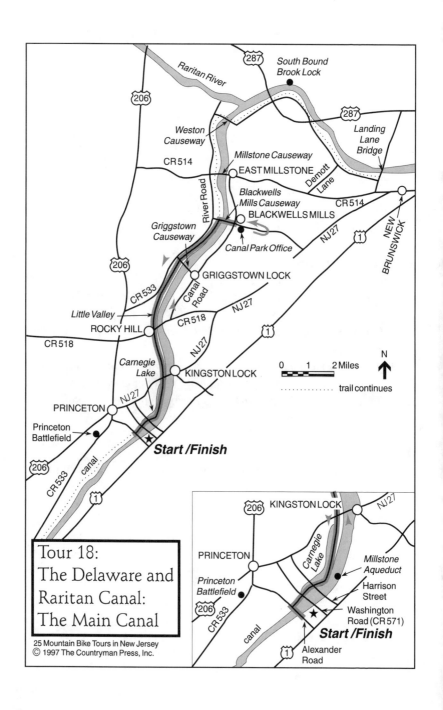

Raritan River

287

South Bound
Brook Lock

206

287

Weston
Causeway

Landing
Lane
Bridge

CR 514

Millstone Causeway

EAST MILLSTONE

Demott
Lane

River Road

Blackwells
Mills Causeway

CR 514

NEW BRUNSWICK

BLACKWELLS MILLS

NJ 27

1

Griggstown
Causeway

Canal Park Office

206

CR 533

Canal Road

GRIGGSTOWN LOCK

Little Valley

CR 518

NJ 27

ROCKY HILL

NJ 27

1

CR 518

Carnegie
Lake

NJ 27

KINGSTON LOCK

0   1   2 Miles

N

trail continues

PRINCETON

NJ 27

Princeton
Battlefield

Start /Finish

206

CR 533

canal

1

**Tour 18:
The Delaware and
Raritan Canal:
The Main Canal**

25 Mountain Bike Tours in New Jersey
© 1997 The Countryman Press, Inc.

206

KINGSTON LOCK

NJ 27

PRINCETON

Carnegie
Lake

Millstone
Aqueduct

Princeton
Battlefield

Harrison
Street

206

CR 533

canal

Washington
Road (CR 571)

Start /Finish

1

Alexander
Road

a municipal park (Turning Basin Park) and picnic area here, as well as a designated canal parking area. This spot is within walking distance of town (1.5 miles). Parking is available in Princeton, too, and it's just a short pedal across Carnegie Lake and back to the path.

The canal lies west of US 1, and just east of downtown Princeton. From the intersection of US 1 and CR 571 (Washington Road), go south on US 1 a distance of 0.5 mile and turn right. This is Alexander Road. In another 0.5 mile you'll find the park.

0.00 *Looking north, with the canal just to your right, start the tour. There are two paths here, one on each side of the canal. You want the one on the west side.*

0.20 *Go under the railroad bridge.*

This is a historic "swing" structure, which was designed to swing aside for canal traffic rather than draw up. The area surrounding the path is a thin wooded buffer. The surface is an easy-riding sandy gravel. Soon, Carnegie Lake will appear to your left (west).

0.60 *Cross Washington Road (CR 571), which is the most direct entry to Princeton.*

If you want to visit, turn left, go over the bridge, and in 0.8 mile you'll reach the downtown area. Town and campus can also be reached from Alexander Road, which turns into Alexander Street after crossing the canal.

Take the opportunity at some point to tour the campus. You can arrange for a free 1-hour tour, or just ride your bike through the university grounds. Tours are run by undergraduates, who discuss the history, academics, and student life of the university. You'll be impressed by the turn-of-the-century collegiate Gothic architecture in the style of Oxford and Cambridge and by the innumerable elegant halls and residences.

The town of Princeton also has a rich history. It served as a temporary meeting place for the Continental Congress. The British surrendered to Washington here. Woodrow Wilson lived here in 1836, as did Albert Einstein from 1932 to 1955. (See the mini-tour of Princeton at the end of this tour.)

Continue north on the canal path.

1.25 Cross Harrison Street.

1.70 Walk your bike across the footbridge at Millstone Aqueduct.

There are excellent views of 3-mile-long Carnegie Lake through this section. Over the bridge and to your right, a footbridge leads to a parking area with sanitary facilities. Trees were cut from the path along this section to allow for effective dredging in 1985. There are benches and scenic stops along the lake's edge.

Continue on, with Carnegie Lake to your left.

Along this section, turn and look west to see the Gothic tower of Holder, a university residence.

3.80 Arrive at Kingston Lock.

Here are excellent examples not only of a lock, but also of a locktender's house and a toll house. There's also a turning basin off the canal, where barges could unload or stop for the night.

Go through the culvert tunnel and bear right back to the path.

Foliage—primarily oak and maple trees with an occasional chestnut and ash and lots of poison ivy—increases as you travel north, and the Millstone River appears to your left, flowing beside the path for most of the distance between Kingston and Rocky Hill.

5.70 Cross CR 518 at Rocky Hill.

A mile before reaching the footbridge and bridle path in Little Valley, look for the concrete halfway mile marker with the inscription 22/22. You're 22 miles in each direction from the extremes of the (original) canal termini. You'll see several markers along the way.

6.70 Pass a footbridge to the road and a path to your left in Little Valley.

The path is a bridle trail that penetrates the Millstone River floodplain.

8.15 Pass Griggstown Lock on your right.

Through this rural area you'll ride adjacent to either the Millstone River or its floodplain. Canal Road, to your right, is a narrow road with historic homes. On the west side of the canal is the busier River Road. Neither is an imposition upon the quiet and removed ambience of the towpath.

8.90 *Arrive at Griggstown Causeway.*

This causeway crosses the canal, connecting Canal Road and River Road. A number of historic buildings can be found here, in addition to parking and picnic areas. The Delaware and Raritan Canal State Park Master Plan says of this spot, "The character of the place as a whole is often cited as the epitome of a preserved 19th-century rural scene." The causeway area was the site of a mill, store, and inn. At places like this, 18th-century farmers brought their produce to load onto freight barges. Lock- and bridgetender's residences, muletender's barracks, and a variety of quaint and antiquated buildings grace the scene. The canal is placid and spotted with colonies of arrowroot. At Griggstown, you begin to feel the true spirit of the times.

To turn around at this point would mean a round trip of nearly 18 miles, a good day's outing—and probably as far as you'd want to travel if you'd like to spend time in Princeton. However, towpath miles tend to be fast miles compared to most off-road rides, and if you feel up to a total round trip of about 25 miles, by all means continue to Blackwells Mills, another 19th-century causeway and similar in character to Griggstown. From there, you can visit the D&R Canal Park Office, where a variety of public information is available, along with sanitary facilities and a telephone.

To extend your trip, then, continue north.

12.65 *At Blackwells Mills Causeway, turn right, cross the canal, turn right onto Canal Road, and go 0.1 mile to the park office on the left.*

Blackwells Mills is another interesting and scenic canal cross-roads, with several 18th- and 19th-century homes and farm-steads facing the canal. It's also near the Millstone River Historic District, a collection of houses and a forge dating from 1700. Of course, Washington stayed here after his victory at Princeton. This historic district isn't centralized, so touring it by bike isn't

147

entirely practical. But for future reference, it lies between Montgomery Township and the Borough of Millstone west of the Millstone River.

Turn around and head south at this point, retracing your path to Alexander Road. Should you wish to explore farther north, by all means do so, but watch that you don't get caught in the dark unprepared.

Just 2 miles north is Millstone Causeway. There's a deli there, as well as an interesting used bookstore, the Franklin Inn. Preservation of this 260-year-old landmark inn, which housed British general Charles Cornwallis in June 1777, is paid for by book sales. It's open Wednesday from noon to 3 PM and weekends from 1 to 4.

Between East Millstone and the canal path's origin at Landing Lane Bridge (about 13 miles), the surface is good and the atmosphere—until you reach several urban transitional zones around South Bound Brook and New Brunswick—is peaceful. This section of trail also has the advantage of being next to the very scenic Raritan River, from just north of Weston Causeway to New Brunswick. There are some outstanding locks and historic structures in this section, but there's also a sudden intrusion of industrial buildings and large roads above Weston.

The Mini-Tour of Princeton

Princeton University is visited by about 27,000 people each year. Most of them participate in the free campus tours that are offered Monday through Saturday at 10, 11, 1:30, and 3:30, and Sunday at 1:30 and 3:30. For information on joining a tour, call the public relations office at 609-258-3603. To tour the campus on your own, follow the directions below. Mileages are approximate.

0.00 *From the towpath at Washington Road (CR 571), go northwest, crossing Carnegie Lake. This will take you through the campus area.*

0.80 *At Nassau Street, you're in the center of Princeton itself. Turn left, following Nassau Street.*

148

Carnegie Lake

1.25 *Arrive at the commemorative Battle Monument, in itself a worthy destination.*

Just to the right are the Princeton town offices (Princeton Battlefield State Park is a mile south of here on CR 533). Go inside and request a map of the Princeton campus. Go back toward town on Nassau Street.

1.40 *Turn right off Nassau Street and enter the campus through the main gate, University Place. This will bring you onto Elm Drive. Bear left and follow south.*

1.90 *At Faculty Road you have a choice. You can turn left (northeast), cross Washington Road, and tour the side of campus in the Palmer Stadium–Saxton Field area by turning left onto FitzRandolph Road, left again onto Prospect Avenue (the designated bike path through town), then making*

another left onto Washington Road and heading back across the lake. Or you can go right (southwest) on Faculty Road and turn left onto Alexander Street to return to your car.

Campus buildings that are open to the public include Nassau Hall (1756) and The Art Museum. Call for information and hours.

Information

D&R Canal State Park
625 Canal Road, Somerset, NJ
732-873-3050

Princeton University Public Relations Department
609-258-3603

Bicycle Repair Services

Jay's Cycles
249 Nassau Street, Princeton, NJ
609-924-7233; 1-800-783-5292

Bike-N-Gear II
Somerset, NJ
732-873-0210

ATLANTIC HIGHLANDS

The Monmouth County Park System

The following three tours—Hartshorne Woods, Huber Woods, and the Henry Hudson Trail—are managed by the Monmouth County Park System, which features what's currently the most organized and progressive multiple-use trail planning in New Jersey. The parks are highly managed for a variety of uses, with trails designated for specific user groups. One result is a high number of satisfied and involved park patrons—and a correspondingly low level of user conflicts.

Another result is a system that functions as a prototype not only for interstate trail planners (and Monmouth does cooperate with other counties in the state on questions of trail use and design), but also for regional and national managers. Indeed, Monmouth's sensible trail management adheres to the same principles advocated by national planners such as the International Mountain Biking Association.

The park system's acquisition and designs department has modified older trails and created new ones to meet the needs of the growing off-road cycling community. Since our impact on the resource is intense, and appropriate design requires sensitivity to environment and topography, the park system employs an ecologist—Ken Thoman—for that purpose.

How refreshing it is to hear a planner advocating management over regulation! Quoting Ken: "It's not the user that's destroying the trails, it's the design that's not appropriate for the user. Trails should be designed accordingly, and management should then inform the user what the intended use is for that particular trail. If park managers have to resort to regulations, management has failed. Regulation is inefficient and requires manpower to enforce it, and regulation is often enforced randomly. We technically don't use regulation in this system unless the whole park is closed, as with some congested urban parks, and even with an estimated 10 percent renegade population, this has proven to be our most effective approach. To convey information—to effectively direct and educate the user—is the key."

No wonder that the Monmouth County Park System is in such good shape—and that it works.

Another reason this county park system (including Allaire State Park and Cheesequake State Park) is in good shape is the NJCCC's volunteer upkeep of trails. Contact the NJCCC for details about their annual work schedule (see Advocacy Groups).

There are 26 parks in the system, and several larger ones that invite off-road bicycle use are not included in this book. It would be worth your time to investigate Shark River Park, Turkey Swamp Park, Clayton Park, and the Manaquan Reservoir Perimeter Trail.

Call or write the park system for information: Monmouth County Park System Public Information Office (908-842-2000), 805 Newman Springs Road, Lincroft, NJ 07738-1695.

19
Henry Hudson Trail

Location: Aberdeen, Middletown, Atlantic Highlands, Monmouth County
Distance: 22.54 miles out and back
Terrain: Flat rail trail
Surface: Cinder, improved surface, paved
Maps: Henry Hudson Trail Map, Monmouth County Park System;
  Monmouth County Map
Highlights: Coastal estuary cycling on easy, scenic surfaces; road
  links to Raritan Bay, nearby Sandy Hook Unit, Gateway National
  Recreation Area, Twin Lights State Historic Site

The Henry Hudson Trail comprises about 9 of the estimated 7100 rail-trail miles in the United States. It serves not only as a recreational path but also as a local thoroughfare for schoolchildren, residents, and commuters. Plans are to connect the trail with the local train stations as well as Sandy Hook and Sea Bright. It passes through several communities along its way, and you can easily leave the trail and ride a short distance to bayshore beaches with public access.

The railbed is that of the former Central Railroad of New Jersey, which carried fishing and building products. (The state continues to be a leading producer of these products because its tax structure is designed to promote industrial development.) The path itself has seen many improvements since its commercial days and is beautifully maintained by the park system, volunteers, and its municipalities. You'll like the bridges, marshes, tidal wetlands, and occasional bay views.

Foot traffic, bicycles, and horses are permitted, but no motorized vehicles are allowed. This is an excellent first ride for small children and their families, as well as for the experienced sightseeing cyclist. Exercise caution at street crossings. Wear a helmet!

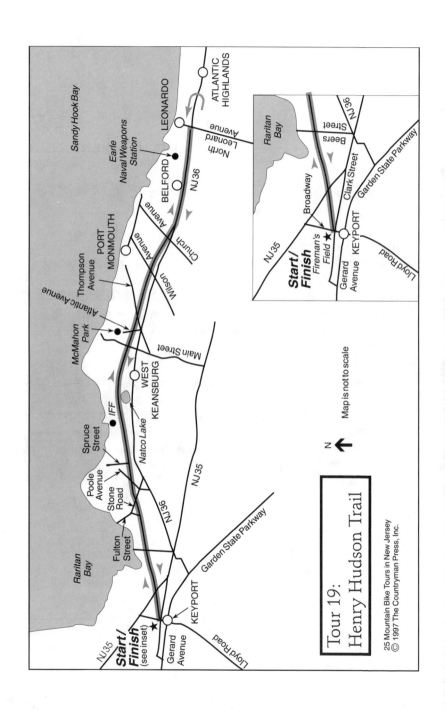

Tour 19:
Henry Hudson Trail

25 Mountain Bike Tours in New Jersey
© 1997 The Countryman Press, Inc.

Map is not to scale

Travel the corridor first from west to east. To reach the west end, take exit 117A off the Garden State Parkway, toward Keyport. The trail access is right off the parkway at the intersection of Lloyd Road, Gerard Avenue, and Clark Street. On the northeast quadrant of this intersection you'll see Fireman's Field. Park there. The trail begins diagonally across Broadway from the field. Look for the trail signs (BAYSHORE TRAIL SYSTEM).

0.00 Get on the cinder right-of-way.

Though this is a congested and populated spot, the atmosphere relaxes considerably as you travel east.

0.26 Cross a bridge over a small creek (Luppatatong Creek).

0.35 Cross NJ 35.

0.64 Cross a paved road (Beers Street).

0.83 Cross Main Street.

0.95 Cross Broad Street.

1.10 Cross Church Road.

1.32 Cross Green Grove Avenue.

1.52 Cross Fulton Street.

There's dense vegetation here. Also, watch for broken glass.

1.75 From a wooden bridge in a tidal marsh you can see bits of Raritan Bay (Keyport Harbor) to your left.

1.84 Cross Stone Road (County Route 6) in a densely foliated residential area.

2.14 Cross Florence Avenue.

2.42 Cross Poole Avenue. The trail becomes a skinny dirt single-track.

2.71 Pass through the back parking lot and playing field area of Memorial School in Union Beach.

2.86 Cross Spruce Street.

2.98 After a wooden bridge in a small residential area, the surface trail widens.

3.19 Cross Union Avenue.

To the left (0.5 mile) is Union Beach. You may see signs for

Jersey Avenue at this point, which runs parallel to the trail here.

3.14 *From a tidal creek with two small bridges you can see the Verrazanno Narrows Bridge that links Staten Island and Brooklyn.*

3.80 *Pass IFF (International Flavors and Fragrances).*

3.90 *On your right is Natco Lake. You're entering West Keansburg.*

4.23 *Cross another small bridge over Thorns Creek.*

There's a marina in the creek, to your left (north).

4.43 *Cross Central Avenue.*

4.58 *Cross Laurel Avenue.*

5.09 *Cross the Waackaack Creek and Creek Road.*

5.15 *Cross Church Street.*

5.41 *Cross (another) Main Street.*

5.90 *Pass McMahon Park on your left.*

6.10 *Cross Atlantic Avenue.*

6.27 *Cross Thompson Avenue.*

6.64 *Cross a bridge.*

7.03 *Cross Bray Avenue.*

7.33 *Cross Wilson Avenue.*

This is the site of the old Port Monmouth Train Station, which is open Wednesdays from 10 AM to noon. Also found here is "Ripper" Collins Park, a memorial to Korean War veterans.

7.80 *Cross Compton Creek.*

7.94 *Cross (another) Church Street.*

8.16 *Cross a third Main Street, this one in Belford.*

8.41 *Cross East Road.*

9.33 *The trail joins NJ 36 here. Pass Earle Naval Weapons Station here.*

9.55 *Cross Broadway.*

9.84 *Cross Appleton Street.*

10.20 *Cross (another) Thompson Avenue.*

Crossing an estuary on the Henry Hudson Trail

10.77 Arrive at North Leonard Avenue.

There's a small memorial to Leonardo's World War II soldiers here, as well as a grocery store and delicatessen.

Turn around here. (The trail continues for another 0.2 mile on a sandy singletrack to a private parking lot and stops there.)

You're about 4 miles west of Sandy Hook and the Gateway National Recreation Area, a great place for road biking.

Information

Monmouth County Park System
Public Information Office,
805 Newman Springs Road, Lincroft, NJ 07738-1695
908-842-4000

Atlantic Highlands

For information about other rail trails in New Jersey:

New Jersey Rail-Trails
PO Box 23, Pluckemin, NJ 07978

For information on the Gateway National Recreation Area:
Visitors Center
732-872-5970

National Park Service
732-872-0115

Bicycle Repair Services

Mike's Bikes
Atlantic Highlands, NJ
732-291-8822

Tom's Atlantic Cyclery
Atlantic Highlands, NJ
732-291-2664

20
Hartshorne Woods Park

Location: *Monmouth County, Middletown*
Distance: *9 miles*
Terrain: *Hilly*
Surface: *Dirt, sand, gravel, pavement*
Maps: *Hartshorne Woods Park Trail Map (free)*
Highlights: *State-of-the-art, multiple-use designed and managed trail system with excellent marking and trailhead information; Battery Lewis historic military site; picnic and viewing areas on the Navesink River; Gateway National Recreation Area, Sandy Hook Unit*

For mountain bikers, Hartshorne Woods Park (pronounced *harts-horne*) is the crown jewel of the Monmouth County Park System. This compact, well-conceived and -designed 11-mile trail system contained within 750 acres may even qualify as the most popular off-road cycling spot in the Atlantic Highlands. It features the park system's convenient trail classification: green circles (easy trails, designated primarily for walking); blue squares (moderately difficult, multiple-use trails, designed and maintained for hikers, equestrians, and all-terrain bicyclists, unless otherwise indicated), and black diamonds (challenging trails with steep grades and possible obstructions, intended for the same users as the blue trails). There are numerous challenging, deep-woods miles to explore and several places to picnic or relax off the paved roads around the Rocky Point Section, on the shores of Navesink River Bay. More attractive road miles surround the park. A good day's worth of riding is possible here, and a quick road connection with Huber Woods (Tour 21) exists should you want to tour both parks in a single day, which many riders do.

To reach the park, take NJ 35 to Navesink River Road (north of Cooper Avenue Bridge in Red Bank). Go east on Navesink River Road

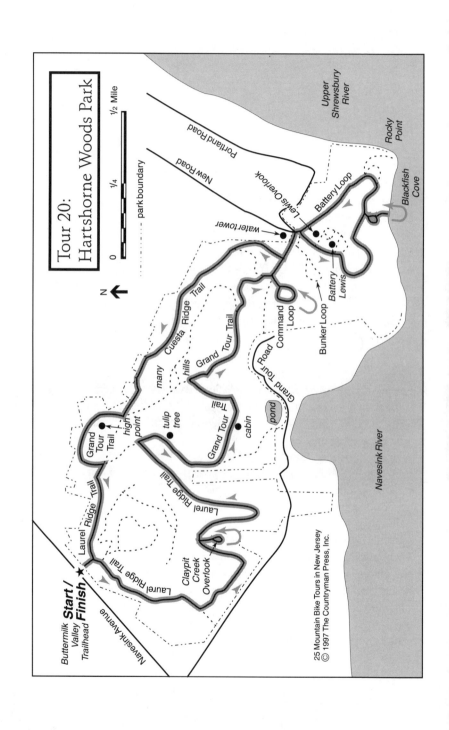

Tour 20:
Hartshorne Woods Park

N

0   ¼   ½ Mile

----- park boundary

Buttermilk **Start /**
Valley **Finish**
Trailhead

Navesink Avenue

Laurel Ridge Trail

Laurel Ridge Trail

Claypit Creek
Overlook

Grand Tour
Trail

tulip
tree

high
point

cabin

pond

many

hills

Cuesta Ridge Trail

Grand Tour Trail

Grand Tour Trail

Grand Tour
Road

Command
Loop

Bunker Loop

Battery
Lewis

Battery Loop

Lewis Overlook

water tower

New Road

Portland Road

Upper
Shrewsbury
River

Rocky
Point

Blackfish
Cove

Navesink River

25 Mountain Bike Tours in New Jersey
© 1997 The Countryman Press, Inc.

(CR 12A). At 2.8 miles you'll pass Brown's Dock Road; continue straight for 1 more mile. Merge with CR 8A as you pass Oceanic Bridge to your right, and turn right onto Locust Avenue at 4.1 miles. Cross Claypit Creek, bear right onto Navesink Avenue in front of a large stone church, and at 5.3 miles, you'll see the park entrance on your right.

Park at the Buttermilk Valley Trailhead and walk your bike through the dismount area to the signboard. This is a popular family destination, and park personnel are very concerned about safety in this area. They request that you walk your bike to and from the trails that depart from here. People congregate in particular around the signboard, which is at the bottom of the hilly Laurel Ridge Trail. Watch for children.

0.00 *Go right onto the Laurel Ridge singletrack trail (blue squares). This is a sandy uphill section.*

0.46 *Turn left at a T.*

0.98 *At a Y, turn right, toward Claypit Creek Overlook.*

1.19 *Arrive at the overlook.*

Views of the Navesink River and valley are limited here during periods of heavy foliage.

1.35 *Back at the Y, turn right.*

Several areas in the park have blocked-off trails. This is to help them recover from erosion as a result of inappropriate use by mountain bikers. The new trails you're riding on, which incorporate pieces of the older ones, are designed for intensive multiple use.

This is a beautiful singletrack descent in a setting of red oak trees with few rocks and occasional log obstructions. The park's management policy keeps some obstructions in place: They slow traffic as well as provide technical challenges.

2.40 *Turn right at a Y onto the Grand Tour Trail (black diamonds).*

The trail goes slightly downhill here through a mature oak forest over a loamy, smooth, well-kept surface. You're heading for the Monmouth Hills Section.

2.53 *Go under a large tulip tree that has blown down over the trail and reestablished itself with a long runner.*

This tree is on the map. Be careful if you decide to side saddle this one: The trunk is at around handlebar height.

2.76 *At a Y, bear right. The trail to the left is vague at this time.*

2.84 *At another Y, go left and uphill. A signpost to your left marks the Grand Tour Trail, but the post is not well oriented.*

There are distant houses to the right through the woods, and the trail going straight (bearing right) is flat and leads to the park maintenance area.

2.96 *Pass a cabin on your right.*

3.34 *At the T, turn right.*

The area to your left is described on the map as having "many hills." (It does.) This loop of the Grand Tour encloses the Monmouth Hills Section.

3.61 *At a Y, bear left and go uphill.*

The right turn here would take you, in 0.04 mile, to a wooden gate and onto Grand Tour Road, the shoreside, scenic, easterly extension of Hartshorne Road.

3.83 *At a Y, go right and climb.*

4.05 *Arrive at a paved road with a pair of cement pillars to your right.*

This is the Rocky Point Section. Directly to your right is a cinder road that goes out to the end of Grand Tour Road, off park property. Next to it, going uphill, is Command Loop.

Go up and ride around the loop, which offers a view in periods of thin foliage.

At this spot, a radar tracking installation served Battery Lewis and later became a Nike-Hercules missile control center to serve the installations at Sandy Hook.

Come back down the hill to the cement pillars.

4.60 *From the cement pillars, continue on the paved road, leaving the trail you came up on to your left.*

4.65 *Pass and take note of the Cuesta Ridge Trail (blue squares) on your left. It's the trail you'll come back on later.*

164

4.70 *Pass the Bunker Loop to your right.*

4.73 *Passing a water tower to your left and reaching the intersection of New Road and Battery Loop, turn right, continuing on a paved road and going past the park signboard to your right. The large mound of earth to your left (east) is Battery Lewis.*

You can take a very short walk to the top, to Lewis Overlook, on a foot trail from the east side of the battery if you're interested. The views of the ocean make it well worth the trip.

This is the World War II emplacement site of two 16-inch guns (16 inches being the diameter of the projectile) that were surplused as a result of the Washington Naval Treaty of 1922. This treaty limited the number of battleships a country could deploy. The guns, which the navy gave to the Highlands Army Air Defense (part of the Atlantic Coast Air Defense System, connected to Fort Hancock on Sandy Hook), were 66 feet long and could fire a 1-ton, armor-piercing round 28 miles—over the horizon. The rounds could go through the deck of a battleship—or "anything that moved," as the army claimed—and explode inside it. Another nearby bunker housed a pair of 6-inch guns, which were for targeting faster-moving ships such as destroyers, minesweepers, PT-type boats, and amphibious landing craft.

Because the United States was never invaded, the coastal defenses in place here were never used, and the battery and its supporting barracks and structures were later dismantled. The big guns were only fired once, in 1943, for testing. People in the area were sent notices warning them to open their doors and windows and take down their china in anticipation of the huge shock wave that would follow the discharges. Then the guns were fired. Windows were still broken in Sea Bright—right under the battery and less than a mile away.

Continue on the paved Battery Loop, keeping the battery to your left, and bear right at the end of the mound. Go downhill.

5.65 *Turn right and descend steeply to Blackfish Cove, where picnic tables and a short pier into the Navesink River greet you.*

This is the best place in the park to have lunch or to take a break. The visit to the cove is worth the paved road you traveled to get here.

Return to Battery Loop. Before leaving it, however, look to your right for a new 1.2-mile-long multiuse trail, which will connect with Rocky Point Road at mileage 6.4 If you choose this detour, disconnect your odometer at 6.4 miles and reconnect it at the top.

6.10 *Turn right onto Battery Loop, going uphill. Bear right, staying on the loop road.*

6.40 *Pass the road down to Rocky Point to your right.*

6.85 *Arrive back at the beginning of Battery Loop. Go straight, leaving the water tower to your right and the Bunker Loop to your left.*

6.95 *Turn right onto the Cuesta Ridge Trail.*

7.97 *At a four-way intersection, turn right onto the Grand Tour Trail toward an area designated as a "high point" on the map. (It is.) Cross a grassy road (not shown on the map), and continue on the singletrack, which roughly parallels the grassy road and then drops away to the northwest and downhill.*

8.10 *Bear left as a small singletrack goes to the right and out of the park.*

8.13 *Cross back over the grassy road. The Grand Tour Trail picks up again straight across this road. Go downhill carefully over some water bars.*

8.45 *At a T, go left. The trail to the right is currently closed. Climb gently.*

8.51 *Arrive at the intersection of the Grand Tour and Laurel Ridge Trails. Turn right.*

9.00 *As you reach the trailhead near the parking area where you began, dismount your bike.*

Huber Woods Connector

To reach Huber Woods from Hartshorne by bike, go back across Claypit Creek on Locust Avenue, turn left onto CR 8A, and pedal 0.1 mile to an unnamed dirt road on the edge of an open field to your right (this point is visible from the left you took onto CR 8A). Turn right and go a few hundred feet to the trailhead on your left. You'll see a park signboard here. This is the (blue) Claypit Run Trail. Use the signboard map to orient yourself (see Tour 21, "Huber Woods"). Future plans include a more direct trail link between these two parks, which will minimize road travel.

Information

Monmouth County Park System
805 Newman Springs Road, Lincroft, NJ 07738-1695
732-842-1695
People with hearing impairments may call TDD 908-219-9484.

Gateway National Recreation Area—Sandy Hook Unit
Visitors Center
732-872-5970

National Park Service
732-872-0115

Bicycle Repair Services

Mike's Bikes
Atlantic Highlands, NJ
732-291-8822

Tom's Atlantic Cyclery
Atlantic Highlands, NJ
732-291-2664

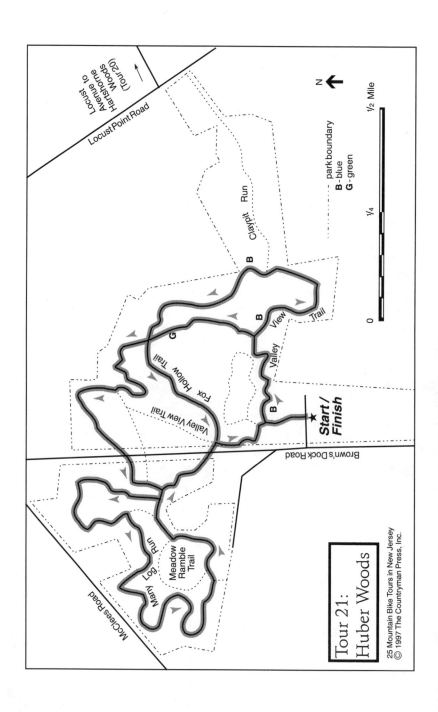

Locust
Avenue to
Hartshorne Woods
(Tour 20)

Locust Point Road

N

park boundary
B - blue
G - green

Claypit Run

0   ¼   ½ Mile

B

B

Valley View Trail

G

Fox Hollow Trail

Valley View Trail

B

Start /
Finish

Brown's Dock Road

Meadow Ramble Trail

Many Log Run

McClees Road

Tour 21:
Huber Woods

25 Mountain Bike Tours in New Jersey
© 1997 The Countryman Press, Inc.

21
Huber Woods

Location: *Monmouth County*
Distance: *4.93 miles, with options for additional miles*
Terrain: *Hilly singletrack trails*
Surface: *Dirt, with log jumps and very few rocks*
Maps: *Huber Woods Park, Monmouth County Park System (free at park)*
Highlights: *Legal, improved singletrack; excellent trail system, environmental center; bicycle access to Hartshorne Woods Park*

Any mountain biker in the Atlantic Highlands will know about Huber Woods. This biker-friendly park offers an outstanding singletrack ride, along with the uncommonly attractive grounds and estate bequeathed by the Huber family. Trails are well marked and well maintained, and the terrain in this heavily wooded section of Middletown consists of gentle hills and well-established dirt surfaces. A strong volunteer corps of trail maintainers and the friendly, supportive staff of the Monmouth County Park System have produced in Huber Woods a cohesive, working model of a multiple-use trail. It's rare to find a facility of this quality that so openly promotes and encourages mountain bikers. Equestrians, walkers, and hikers are also encouraged.

It's not surprising that James Fenimore Cooper himself spoke of the Navesink highlands as "one of the most beautiful combinations of land and water in America"—unless, of course, you've visited his native Hudson Valley—and it remains as beautiful in our day. There are still the expansive views Cooper saw, along with newer Mediterranean-style villas, English Tudor mansions, and manor houses reminiscent of northern European architecture, which dot the yacht-infested waters from Rumson to Red Bank. Early guidebook writers described carriage tours around the countryside and through the local villages. Sloops and steamboats carried passengers, news, and produce to New York City on regular schedules from the 1820s; yacht clubs held formal races from 1900.

Among the early entrepreneurs of the period was Joseph Huber, who came to America in 1833 and built the German-Swiss manor house that's now the park's environmental center, an impressive structure of brick with half-timbering, a turret, and three solid chimneys. You can go through it during regular business hours and weekends. Rangers and staff members are on site to assist you.

The park has other attractions, including an equestrian center, a reptile house, a weather station, a bird-viewing area, classrooms, and a discovery path (both this and the Equestrian Program Center are accessible to people with disabilities), plus, of course, telephones and rest rooms. Groups are welcomed, and interpretive programs are offered. There's plenty to occupy the nonrider who might want to come along with you.

There are 6 miles of trail here, and all-terrain bicycles are allowed on most of them. A large and comprehensive signboard at the trailhead will direct you to the legal trails. The most popular area of the park for mountain bikers is without doubt—and for obvious reasons—the trail named Many Log Run, west of Brown's Dock Road. You access it from the main trail system near the parking lot. Many Log Run is informally maintained as a technical singletrack, although not a difficult one, and it represents an opportunity for the advancing rider to try new skills on what is essentially forgiving terrain with long, gliding flats, short climbs and pitches, and wild, smooth curves through dense and tightly packed hardwoods with—in several cases—limited forward vision. Adroit, off-the-seat handling, static jumps, and moving leaps with some sudden, short-cornering skills are required for handling the trails and some of the log jumps here. Naturally, you can also walk or ride around log jumps and slow down in the narrows and curves, according to your ability level. You won't learn advanced technique without pushing yourself somewhat, but do this safely, and only with the full understanding of the new skill and its execution and—ideally—with the company of a rider who has already mastered and can demonstrate the skills. Be careful, and watch for trail traffic, which will invariably contain fast-moving riders coming at you. Helmets are highly recommended.

To reach the park, take NJ 35 to Navesink River Road (north of

Cooper Avenue Bridge in Red Bank), go east on Navesink River Road 2.8 miles, and turn left on Brown's Dock Road. In 0.3 mile you'll see the park entrance to your right. Huber Woods Park is open from 8 AM to dusk every day of the year, free of charge.

From a deck just east of the parking area you can get a view of the Navesink River. The Navesink (pronounced *nav-sink*) is Monmouth County's largest watershed, a broad and shallow river about a mile wide but only 5.5 miles in length. Coursing amid the scenic highlands and elegant shore homes of Rumson Neck, the river joins Sandy Hook Bay in the town of Atlantic Highlands. The Navesink is an important estuary for indigenous populations of fish, clams, oysters, and mussels, species that formed the foundation of the area's early economy. The popular Shrewsbury and Navesink varieties of oysters were farmed here. When these beds became overfished around 1800, they were actually replanted with oysters brought from the tidewaters of Virginia and Long Island Sound. The industry finally succumbed around 1920 to disease, overharvesting, and pollution. With tightening standards, however, this important estuarine habitat is a productive nursery for many fish species.

0.00 *From the parking area, follow the thin dirt trail across the north lawn and into the woods.*

0.08 *The signboard is here. Turn right onto Valley View Trail (blue).*

0.34 *At a T, turn right.*

0.63 *At a Y, go left.*

Claypit Run goes off to the right, leading eventually to Locust Point Road. You can go over to Hartshorne Woods this way.

0.99 *At a T, bear left. The right turn leads to private property.*

1.03 *Intersect with the Fox Hollow Trail and bear right, staying on the blue trail.*

1.05 *Continue on the blue trail at a Y.*

1.32 *At the intersection of three trails (the trail to the right is fenced off), take the middle trail (blue). Keep bearing left through this section as smaller trails come in from the right.*

1.57 *At Brown's Dock Road, go straight across and continue on the trail.*

1.71 At a T, go straight. A small singletrack goes to your left.

1.73 Go right at a T, leaving the blue trail that heads left.

1.75 At a T, go right onto Many Log Run.

2.02 Pass a small singletrack on your right (Brown's Dock Road is a few hundred feet to your right here).

2.05 Pass a singletrack on your right.

2.24 Bear right at a Y.

2.32 At a T bear right and go uphill, passing a residential neighborhood to your right.

2.66 Continue straight through a four-way intersection. There's a trail post here with a black-diamond marker ("challenging"). Go slightly downhill from here.

3.16 At a Y, go left.

3.18 Reaching an intersection within view of the last Y, go straight (right). Many Log Run goes off to the left.

3.22 Cross a meadow with a residence to your right.

3.34 Go straight. As the trail enters the woods here, another small trail goes to your left. You can add 0.6 mile by following this blue trail (Meadow Ramble).

3.38 At a Y, go right, continuing on the Meadow Ramble Trail. The black-diamond trail goes left here.

3.45 Bear right at a Y.

3.47 At a T, go right into a laurel woods. There are several holly trees at this intersection.

3.64 Cross Brown's Dock Road here.

3.67 Cross a fire road, following blue markers.

3.70 At a Y, bear right, staying on the blue trail.

3.88 Arrive back at the signboard where you began. Go straight.

4.13 At a T, go left onto the Fox Hollow trail (green dots).

4.42 Bear left at the intersection with the Valley View trail.

4.44 At a Y, go left.

4.75 *Go left at a four-way intersection. The fire road, which you crossed at 3.67 miles, is visible ahead of you from here. A signpost at this point reads* VALLEY VIEW *and* FOX HOLLOW.

4.78 *At a Y, bear left.*

4.85 *Turn right at the signboard where you began.*

4.93 *Arrive at the parking lot.*

Bicycle Repair Services

Mike's Bikes
Atlantic Highlands, NJ
732-291-8822

Tom's Atlantic Cyclery
Atlantic Highlands, NJ
732-291-2664

COASTAL PLAIN

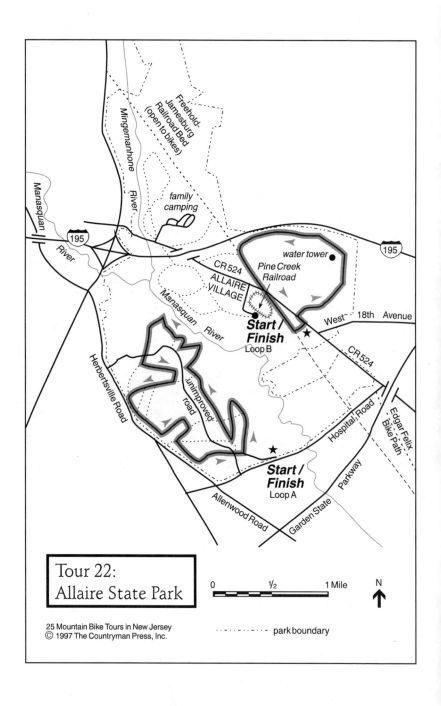

Freehold-
Jamesburg
Railroad Bed
(open to bikes)

Mingemanhone
River

Manasquan
River

195

family
camping

water tower ●

CR 524
ALLAIRE
VILLAGE

Pine Creek
Railroad

195

West   18th   Avenue

CR 524

**Start /
Finish**
Loop B

★

Manasquan
River

Herbertsville Road

unimproved
road

Hospital Road

Edgar Felix
Bike Path

★

**Start /
Finish**
Loop A

Allenwood Road

Garden State
Parkway

Tour 22:
Allaire State Park

0   ½   1 Mile

N
↑

25 Mountain Bike Tours in New Jersey
© 1997 The Countryman Press, Inc.

············· park boundary

22

Allaire State Park

Location: Town of Farmingdale, Monmouth County
Distance: Loop A, 7.54 miles; Loop B, 2.9 miles
Terrain: Flat to slightly hilly
Surface: Park loops are sand, dirt, and gravel
Maps: Allaire State Park, State Park Service map (free); USGS
    Farmingdale, Asbury Park
Highlights: Camping, canoeing, nature center, bridle paths; restored
    19th-century Allaire Village, Pine Creek Railroad; children's playground;
    Spring Meadow Golf Course; proximity to Manasquan Reservoir (5-
    mile loop ride) and Edgar Felix Bike Path (8-mile round trip)

This is one of the more popular places to ride in the New Jersey coastal plain. At only 3068 acres—on the small side for state parks in South Jersey—Allaire has more than its share of interesting multiple-use trails and dirt roads open to the all-terrain cyclist. The trail surfaces that plague larger southern parks such as Wharton and Lebanon State Forests—the dreaded "sugar sand"—are not as problematic here, although you will encounter some deep sand and loam soils, as well as an unusual type of tunneling erosion concentrated right in the middle of the trail. Horses are permitted here, and they prefer the middle of a trail, which further loosens the primary tread surface; bikers, seeking the harder stuff, ride to the sides. The result can be a fairly loose surface, but this varies season-ally and intensifies during times of peak use. The surface rides best when it's frozen.

Other excellent areas to ride are found between Allaire and the Monmouth County parks to the north, and there are a few, excellent flat rides in the immediate vicinity, features that suggest that this state park could make a good base of operations for further exploration. Combined with its period restoration of the old Howell Works (now known as Allaire Village), the adjoining Spring Meadow Golf Course, and an excellent family campsite, an extended stay in this attractive, peaceful park is worth considering.

To reach the park, take exit 31B off I-195 and go east on CR 524. Don't enter by the main entrance, where there's a parking fee for those who come to tour the village. Instead, continue past it for 1.5 miles and take the first right turn after the golf course onto Hospital Road. Go 1.2 miles. Don't park in the first small parking area on your right where Hospital Road crosses the Manasquan River; instead, keep going to the large parking lot, with room for about 100 cars, that's also on your right.

If you're coming from the Garden State Parkway, take exit 98 and follow signs to Allaire State Park. Watch for Hospital Road on your left after turning right onto CR 524.

Loop A

A word of caution: There are so many trails in this circuit, which is commonly referred to as the Horse Trail, that it's easy to get lost. Trails and paths of every description leave from the main trail and are easy to confuse with it. Marking is inconsistent, and cyclometer readings will vary. (If yours is marked in tenths, it won't conform to these, which are given in hundredths.) Ultimately, you should rely on the markers, but failing that, don't be too concerned about getting lost. Though from many points the area seems endless, there are several natural and man-made borders (Hospital Road, Herbertsville Road, and the Manasquan River) you can use to reorient yourself.

0.00 Leave the parking lot from the west end, where the trail departs to the left of a signboard. Trail markers are orange with white arrows and are irregularly posted. This is a narrow, sandy singletrack.

0.05 Cross an unimproved road.

0.30 Cross an old paved road and reenter the woods.

0.37 At a four-way intersection, the horse (multiuse) trail goes in both directions. Go straight.

0.76 At an intersection, continue straight, following arrows through laurel tunnels and up and down hills on a narrow dirt-and-sand singletrack.

1.00 Turn left at a Y where the trail is blocked off ahead, and climb a sandy trench.

1.10 Go through an intersection and climb again.

1.39 At a T at the top of a hill, go right.

2.20 Go left at a three-way marked junction.

2.47 Go straight through an intersection.

2.56 Turn hard right, heading uphill.

2.73 Turn sharp left and go downhill.
Pine trees appear here.

2.85 Bear into the woods again, keeping to the trail, which now approaches a little clearing on a flat singletrack.

3.27 Cross a sand road and continue, watching markers carefully. Go uphill.

3.45 In view of the high-voltage transmission lines, turn left. Watch for glass on the trail.

3.65 Go through an intersection.

4.13 Turn right.

4.40 Pass a trail on your left.

4.58 Go through another intersection.

4.72 Turn left. You can hear cars on Herbertsville Road from here.

4.85 At a four-way intersection, go straight. From this point, the road is to your right about *300* feet away.

5.29 Turn left.

5.60 Go left again. Keep an eye on the markers through here.

5.70 Turn right.

5.78 Go right again.

6.12 Bear left. The road is to your right.

Allaire Village—Please walk your bike.

6.27 *A path departs to the left. Go straight.*

6.30 *A path departs to the right. Continue straight.*

6.38 *You'll see a large sandpit in front of you. Bear left, following the trail, keeping the sandpit to your right.*

6.64 *On the trees to your left, markers indicate somewhat*

vaguely that you should go straight (bear right) instead of turning left here, although most of the impact seems to be going left. Go right, staying on the horse trail. You will see markers.

6.80 Go left.

6.85 Turn left off a broken road surface.

6.96 Go right onto a singletrack.

6.97 Turn right again onto another singletrack.

7.17 Arrive back at the same intersection you passed at the 0.37-mile point. You can turn right here and retrace your route back to the parking lot, or you can follow the unimproved road, passing the model plane field and navigating your way back to the parking lot easily.

7.54 Arrive at the parking lot.

Loop B

There are a few other areas to ride in the park. This loop, also a horse trail, has a harder surface and is almost impossible to get lost on. It's all doubletrack trail. To reach it, park in the designated lot just west of the golf course (toward the main park entrance) on CR 524, near its intersection with the west end of 18th Avenue. Head out of the parking lot, turn left, and ride the shoulder of CR 524. On a nice day you'll see other cyclists riding this good shoulder. Traffic is generally slow and forgiving.

0.00 Within sight of the parking area, turn right onto the horse trail.

0.50 At a Y, bear left, following markers.

1.00 Cross a small creek.

1.30 Pass a water tower on your left. Descend.

1.52 At a T, with the road (I-195) to your right, go straight. Soon you'll see the Freehold-Jamesburg railroad bed (no tracks) to your right, which you ride parallel for about 0.5 mile.

2.28 Reaching CR 524, carefully cross over and turn left on the

grass, in view of the Pine Creek Railroad tracks that go to Allaire Village.

You're just north of the village now, which is nearly in sight. Although it's not permitted to ride your bike in the village itself, you could take a detour here and walk your bike or lock it up so you can look around. Get there by following the tracks in either direction. You're asked not to cross the tracks.

Proceed to your left over a slightly worn path between a row of spruce trees, keeping CR 524 to your left.

2.65 Arrive at a dirt road intersection with steel gates. Allaire Village is to your right. The county road is to the left. Go straight.

2.80 Turn left off the dirt road and onto a path that will lead you up to the parking area.

2.90 Arrive at the parking area.

There are several dirt roads of interest in the park, which can be accessed from the family campground on both sides of the highway and CR 524, as well as a series of trails, most of them for hikers only. Another path to explore is the Freehold-Jamesburg rail trail (see the map in this book to reach it).

While you're here, take a ride on the paved Edgar Felix Bike Path, which runs from Hospital Road (right across from the Manasquan Water Supply) 4 miles southeast to Manasquan. Also worth investigating is a flat, multiuse loop around the Manasquan Reservoir, which is just west of Allaire State Park in Howell Township, east of US-9 and I-195. The area is popular with birders. Birdbiking?

Note: Recently the management of Allaire State Park has been implementing a master plan. ATUG, the Allaire Trail User Group, will be instrumental in the designation, rebuilding, and repair of certain sections of the multi-use area through 1999. This may warrant temporary closings, so be sure to call ahead concerning the park's schedule.

Information

Allaire State Park
PO 220, Farmingdale, NJ 07727
732-938-2371

Manasquan Reservoir
732-919-0996

Bicycle Repair Services

Brielle Cyclery West
Howell, NJ
732-840-9447

Bicycle World, Inc.
Howell, NJ
732-431-5610

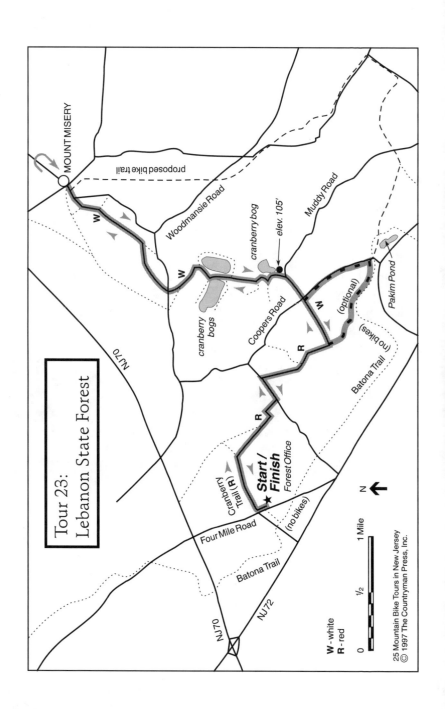

TOUR 23:
Lebanon State Forest

MOUNT MISERY

proposed bike trail

Woodmansie Road

cranberry bog

cranberry bogs

elev. 105'

W

W

Coopers Road

Muddy Road

W

R

(optional)

Batona Trail
(no bikes)

Pakim Pond

NJ70

R

R

Cranberry
Trail (R)

Start /
Finish

Forest Office

(no bikes)

Four Mile Road

Batona Trail

NJ70

NJ72

N

W - white
R - red

0   ½   1 Mile

25 Mountain Bike Tours in New Jersey
© 1997 The Countryman Press, Inc.

23
Lebanon State Forest

Location: *New Lisbon, Burlington County*
Distance: *11.2 miles round trip*
Terrain: *Flat*
Surface: *Firm sand*
Maps: *Lebanon State Forest State Parks Service map (free), park bike path maps (various), USGS Browns Mills (for Cranberry Trail and White Trail), Whiting (for Whitesbog)*
Highlights: *Cabin and tent camping; picnicking, swimming, horse trails; scenic cranberry bog and pine barrens*

In most respects unlike any other part of New Jersey, the Pine Barrens seem part of another world. Long, flat sand roads penetrate dense forests of dwarfed oak and pine for tens of miles, and it's rare to find a local woodsman or forest ranger who can tell you their final destinations. Deep swamps and stands of coveted Atlantic white cedar populate the margins of wetlands and creek branches, creating habitat for several threatened and endangered species. Ponds and south-flowing rivers with a variety of fish, birds, and aquatic plant communities are routine, but most unexpected to visitors new to the Pine Barrens are the scenic and colorful cranberry bogs, which by season's end embrace all the colors of a New England autumn.

And that's the best time to bike Lebanon State Forest and other Barrens tracts, because the summer months are notoriously hot and buggy. If you're not careful, you can end up miles from your intended destination. You'll need to carry extra water, preferably in a backpack-type hydration system, and extra food. If you get "the bug" and become serious about Barrens exploring, you'll need topographic maps, which are available at the park office.

The question of how to approach bicycle touring in a park with *400 miles* of sand roads and an as-yet-uncalculated mileage of legal trails is inherently moot—you get on your bike and ride. (Just stay off the Batona Trail, which is strictly for hiking.) That's one approach. Another is on prescribed bike routes: Park management has acknowledged the growing interest in cycling, both on and off road, by designating several of these. Until you become familiar with the terrain, using these tours is the best approach.

Or you can try the following tours. It has generally been my strategy in this guidebook to create a perimeter tour, introducing you to a general area and its potential for extended touring, but in the case of Lebanon State Forest the perimeter is too big for that. What I've described instead are tours through representative Pine Barrens topography, including the best of those remarkable half-wild, highly manipulated ecosystems, the cranberry bogs—some of which look every bit like backwoods Adirondack ponds. Without a look at the bogs, no tour of southern New Jersey is complete, and after seeing my share, I promise you that the Lebanon bogs are the most accessible and extensive examples on state land.

What no one can do, however, is provide failsafe directions for the bogs themselves. As in any true odyssey, I can bring you to the edge, but then you must go alone. You'll need good maps (but see below), maybe a compass, and an uncanny sense of direction. While most bog roads are laid out in a loose grid fashion, many meander willfully in and out of the surrounding woods, sometimes submerging beneath dank, brown cedar water, others simply disintegrating into an indistinct miasma of mush, alders, and scrub. While it's always reliable to navigate by retracing your route, it's also hard to retain a clear idea of your exact location relative to the trail while doing so. Because of the technological lag (the newest maps date from 1957), all map navigation is, well, hypothetical; the park map gives you only major roads and reference points. Still, all of this may be appropriate: As a neophyte bog biker you'll soon become acquainted firsthand with the tried-and-true cliché that must have had its etymological origins right here in South Jersey: Don't get bogged down. But if you do . . .

It has occurred to many backcountry users that this vast open country could be effectively navigated by handheld GPSs (global positioning sensors), and, indeed, these tools may have more useful applications for cyclists here than in any other part of the state trail system. Still, their accuracy is questionable and their price tag high, and they don't work under trees. If you have one, bring it. If you don't, just think of them as excess baggage and you'll feel better. And if you've never used that fancy wristwatch compass of yours, you'll justify its existence here.

In the end, though, topos and good sense are adequate for navigating the bogs, and the trail described here is marked and self-guiding.

The main entrance to the forest is about 20 miles west of Toms River on NJ 72, roughly 1 mile east of the traffic circle where NJ 70 and NJ 72 meet. The park's northern zone abuts Fort Dix Military Reservation. It's east of Greenwood Forest and north of Wharton State Forest. Other than that, the approximate general location—with due respect to its inhabitants, and from this New Yorker's perspective—is "the middle of nowhere." Welcome to the Barrens.

The Cranberry Trail (red markers, handicapped accessible)

Begin from the parking lot at the forest office. To your right, or east as you face the front entrance of the park office, is Four Mile Road.

0.00 Turn left onto Four Mile Road.

0.80 Turn right onto the red trail, where you see ROAD CLOSED signs.

0.96 At a four-way intersection, follow left, then bear right onto a wide sandy road.

1.27 Go left onto a sand road.

1.52 The red trail goes into the woods through a gate with ROAD CLOSED signs.

1.90 At a Y (elevation 103 feet) bear right.

2.25 The red trail joins the white trail at this point. Go left, onto the white trail.

2.95 Carefully following the white markers that appear on the right side of the road, you'll reach an intersection with Muddy Road. Turn left onto a narrow sand road here (it's at elevation mark 105' on the map). Shortly, you'll enter the bogs.

3.21 At an intersection of trails, bear left.

3.26 Bear right at an intersection and pull out across a bog.

3.49 At a T, with a large bog to the right, go straight.

You can try your hand at exploring now, but return to this point.

3.60 At a T, go straight, crossing a causeway that usually has water on both sides. Keep following white markers.

3.82 At a Y, bear right.

3.86 Bear left onto a narrower, pine-needle-covered trail tunneled in with brush.

4.10 Turn right on a wider sand path. Watch those white markers carefully.

4.19 At a Y, turn right, continuing on a sandy path.

4.24 Cross Woodmansie Road. Pick up the trail directly across the road.

4.77 Go straight across a small sand crossroad. Watch the markers now, and use the trail to guide you. There are many other trails and turns here to confuse you.

4.92 At a T, go left.

5.00 At a four-way intersection, go straight.

5.13 Go straight through another intersection.

5.40 At a Y, bear left. The trail straightens.

5.53 Watch carefully and follow the trail as it branches off to the right. White markers are adequate, but you have to search for them.

5.56 Turn right onto a wider sand road. You'll see a few residences.

5.60 At a dirt road, turn left.

This is Mount Misery. Though aptly described by park superintendent Mr. Christian M. Bethmann as "neither a mountain nor particularly miserable," there is some notable elevation gain (a whole 60 feet) to the south, where there are also opportunities for biking on the higher, denser soils, and where a local off-

A duster lifts off for the cranberry bogs near Lebanon State Forest.

road cycling group holds events. There are proposals to continue the white trail south through this area in the future, to loop back to Pakim Pond, a 5-acre former cranberry reservoir. Navigate your way to Pakim (Lenape for "cranberry") Pond on your return trip by turning south on Coopers Road; from Pakim you can get back on the red trail and return to the park office.

There are bathrooms, water, and (usually) swimming available. There's also a Methodist Conference Center here.

Two park-designed bike routes follow paved or hard sand roads. Request these at the office if you're interested. If you've discovered an affinity for bogs, the best ones—with the longest sand roads—are over at Whitesbog, which is 3 miles north of Mount Misery off—you guessed it—Cranberry Road (CR 530). You can extend your tour from the white trail considerably by cycling to this little-known 1870s cranberry village (currently under restoration), which is also known as the home of the cultivated blueberry, and was at one time the largest cranberry farm in the state. Aside from touring the village, you can tour the bogs for miles, using your topo map . . . and a little imagination. Just watch out for that Jersey Devil who, I'm told, retired to these parts.

Information

Lebanon State Forest
PO Box 215, New Lisbon, NJ 08064
609-726-1191

Whitesbog Preservation Trust
609-893-4646

Bicycle Repair Services

Mount Holly Bicycles
Mount Holly, NJ
609-267-6620

Bike Line
Medford, NJ
609-654-6868

24
Wharton State Forest

Location: Hammonton, Burlington County
Distance: 12.4 miles
Terrain: Pine Barrens, flat
Surface: Sand
Maps: Wharton State Forest, State Park Service map (free) USGS
  Atsion, Jenkins, Chatsworth
Highlights: Batsto Historic Village; wilderness and developed campsites;
  cabins; fishing, boating, canoeing, swimming; bridle paths

The strange beauty of the Pine Barrens comes as a surprise to first-time visitors, and the sheer size of the actual ecosystem, at 1.1 million acres (almost a fifth of New Jersey), is unimaginable. The largest tract of open space between Richmond and Boston, the Pine Barrens was the first area to be designated an international Biosphere Reserve by the United Nations in 1979. And it's not actually barren, obviously; early settlers just called it that because they couldn't grow familiar crops there. These folks had little use for wilderness except to subdue it (how they would marvel at us). In fact, it hosts diverse and abundant flora and fauna, including 100 or more threatened or endangered species, a few species of carnivorous plants, a healthy population of white-tailed deer and lesser mammals (although the bear, panther, timber wolf, and bobcat once found here are gone), and 84 species of breeding birds. It's not unusual to see bald eagles winging over the pines or hunkering down to pick over a carcass in midtrail. There are cedar swamps, savannas, cranberry lands, renegade blueberry patches from early commercial fields, and dozens of other herbaceous plant species. Heath plains of stunted, 4-foot pines cover thousands of acres, with Conrad crowberry and bearberry undergrowth. There are historic settlements, ghost towns, estab-

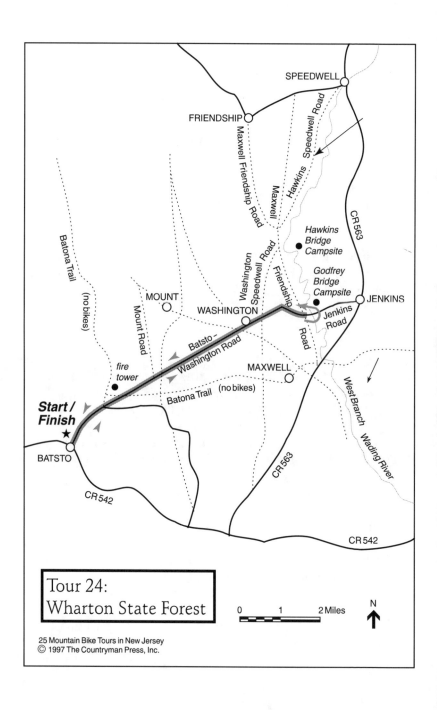

SPEEDWELL

FRIENDSHIP

Maxwell Friendship Road

Maxwell

Hawkins

Speedwell Road

CR 563

Hawkins
Bridge
Campsite

Godfrey
Bridge
Campsite

JENKINS

Batona Trail

(no bikes)

MOUNT

Mount Road

Washington

Speedwell Road

Friendship

Road

Jenkins
Road

WASHINGTON

Batsto –
Washington Road

fire
tower

MAXWELL

Batona Trail   (no bikes)

West Branch

Wading River

**Start /
Finish**

BATSTO

CR 542

CR 563

CR 542

Tour 24:
Wharton State Forest

0   1   2 Miles

N

lished natural areas, long and slow rivers popular with canoeists, and an open, bright forest of dwarfed pine and oak, 109,000 acres of which comprise Wharton State Forest.

The challenge is how to see these Barrens. The problem is their size and their sugar sand. This soft, fluffy sand is the only obstacle to a full tour of the inner Barrens, which is often impassable even to the most able, terrain-trashing four-wheel-drive vehicles—which, crazy as it may seem, are allowed to go just about anywhere in the park. Though their traffic is sparse, their impact is great, and the result is a deeply furrowed, churned-up surface impossible to walk across comfortably, let alone cycle. A sand road may start out looking good and support your weight for a mile or so; then it'll suddenly bury your wheels and leave you in deep . . . sand, unable to move, bug swarmed and sweaty, hoping the situation will improve. But normally it doesn't. There is a way, however, to avoid all this, and it means sticking to major sand roads, which can support your bike. There are several that ply their way deep into the forest.

This tour begins and ends at restored Batsto Village, a large 19th-century bog-iron town, worth a visit in itself. Typically, this South Jersey bog-iron business, which supplied a great deal of hardware and weaponry to the colonial war machine, succumbed to the cheaper, higher grades of ore being mined in Pennsylvania. Batsto then shifted to glass and brick manufacture, since all the ingredients were there—and then it just faded away. Joseph Wharton ("last of the Batsto barons"), an industrialist and gentleman farmer, purchased Batsto and its surrounding tract and subsequently left it undeveloped. It sat until it was scrutinized by the federal government for the creation of a jetport. Under the leadership of Governor Alfred E. Driscoll, Wharton Tract was purchased by the state in 1954.

The forest is about 20 miles northwest of Atlantic City, 40 miles southwest of Philadelphia, and is within easy access of the Atlantic City Expressway, the Garden State Parkway, and US 30 and 206. Try to time your visit with good shore weather, when local use is low. The crowds appear when the Atlantic Ocean is too cold for swimming but the air is still warm enough for camping and "four-wheelin'."

Park at Batsto Village and request a map at the visitors center, which has an excellent small museum and a variety of publications. Be sure to purchase topographic maps if you're at all interested in exploring beyond this text, and always take plenty of food and water with you, particularly in the hot, dry months. It's helpful to talk with staff members and rangers familiar with the area, but do accept a word of caution: Don't take anybody's advice on the condition or ridability of the trails off-road. Only you can determine what's suitable for you, and otherwise well-meaning people who may in fact never have biked the Pine Barrens may send you into a veritable sand trap. I'm speaking from experience. This is wonderful territory and hikes well enough, but it's hell on wheels.

Head out of the parking lot.

0.00 *Turn left onto Batsto–Washington Road.*

0.20 *The Batona Trail crosses the road here (hiking only).*

0.40 *Pass a fire tower to your left.*

0.90 *At an intersection, go straight, leaving the pavement for a sand road (elevation: 32').*

A smaller woods road goes to the left here. You'll see several roads off the main road; some look good enough to ride. Batsto–Washington Road is shaded and level, with little sand drag. In very few places is there enough sand to stall your front wheel; if so, keep your weight off the bars and concentrated over the saddle.

2.50 *Go through a four-way intersection with Mount Road. (Mount Road looks hard enough to ride.)*

4.70 *Arrive at Washington crossroads, another four-way intersection. There's nothing else here at benchmark 55 except a minor stone ruin to the right a few hundred feet southeast on Iron Pipe Road.*

5.20 *Cross Washington Speedwell Road at a four-way intersection. Continue straight.*

6.20 *Cross Maxwell Friendship Road at elevation 42' and go straight; however, you have some other options at this four-way intersection.*

There's a matrix of firm sand roads to your left, in an area between the West Branch and Maxwell Friendship Road; they're unmarked and meandering and tend to dead-end at the river.

Roughly 2 miles or less north of the present intersection, fol-

Jim Burd and Dick Fopeano take a break from paddling the Wading River.

lowing Maxwell Friendship Road, there's a very attractive prim-
itive campsite called Hawkins Bridge, which appears to be little
used. It's possible to continue north into bog country and the
Chatsworth Woods on fair-quality sand from Hawkins Bridge,
crossing the West Branch and continuing on Eagle Road, which
terminates on the USGS Chatsworth map after many northward

miles. I can't vouch for this route's character north of Hawkins Speedwell Road, which turns northeast about 0.8 mile above Hawkins Bridge.

However, Hawkins Speedwell itself also offers a decent surface and can be taken another 3 miles to the intersection of CR 563. A return trip to Jenkins to link with Batsto–Washington Road is practical but ill advised since traffic is fast and shoulders are poor; I recommend a return trip on sand, possibly via Swamp Road, though my experience in the Barrens has taught me to avoid places with names like that.

6.60 *Arrive at the Godfrey Bridge Campsite area, which is loosely clustered around the Wading River.*

There's a water pump and picnic tables here, as well as river access. The campsite extends along the riverbank and Maxwell Friendship Road, with many obscure and private sites. There's a boisterous private campground across the river with a public phone and soda machine. To reach it, cross the bridge and follow Jenkins Road, bearing left into the main entrance.

To complete this tour, return the way you came.

But take some time to explore the countless side roads. There are several other good sand roads in the forest, and you'll get a feel for them after looking around for a few days. Excellent developed campsites with road access exist, particularly at Atsion, and even the Godfrey and Hawkins Bridge Campsites can be reached by car. Several interior sites can be reached only by hiking and canoeing, or on horseback. Call ahead. Permits to camp are required. For additional hard sand road rides, visit nearby Penn State Forest (inquire at Batsto for directions).

Information

Wharton State Forest
RD 9, Batsto, Hammonton, NJ 08037
609-561-0024

Historic Batsto Village
609-561-3262

Atsion Office
609-268-0444

Bicycle Repair Services

Pro Pedals Bike Shop
Hammonton, NJ
609-561-3030

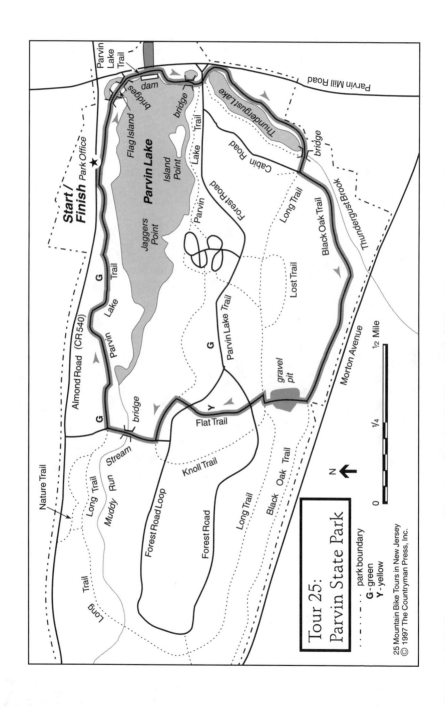

Start / Finish · Park Office

Parvin Lake Trail

dam

bridges

Flag Island

bridge

Parvin Lake

Island Point

Jaggers Point

Parvin Lake Trail

Thunderguist Lake

Parvin Mill Road

bridge

Cabin Road

Forest Road

Long Trail

Black Oak Trail

Thunderguist Brook

Almond Road (CR 540)

Parvin Lake Trail

G

G

G

Lost Trail

gravel pit

bridge

Flat Trail

Y

Knoll Trail

Morton Avenue

Nature Trail

Long Trail

Muddy Run

Stream

Forest Road Loop

Forest Road

Long Trail

Black Oak Trail

Long Trail

N

0   ¼   ½ Mile

Tour 25:
Parvin State Park

25 Mountain Bike Tours in New Jersey
© 1997 The Countryman Press, Inc.

· · · · park boundary
G - green
Y - yellow

25
Parvin State Park

Location: *Elmer Township, Salem County*
Distance: *4.37 miles, with additional unmarked legal mileage available*
Terrain: *Flat*
Surface: *Dirt, hard sand, broken pavement*
Maps: *Parvin State Park, State Park Service map (free), Parvin State Park Appreciation Committee map (most accurate)*
Highlights: *Nature programs; natural-area fishing, boat rentals, swimming; picnicking, camping, cabins; access for people with disabilities*

Small and out-of-the-way—and, as a result, overlooked by all but the most local bikers—this comely and peaceful forest of the southern coastal plain deserves its nickname as the "hidden jewel among New Jersey's parks." Its flat, narrow woods roads and singletrack trails are ideal for beginners and nature lovers and suitable for any rider who wants to get away from it all and fade into anonymity for a while. Families with young children will have the perfect proving ground for the child with that new all-terrain bicycle or hand-me-down cross bike. Anybody with a tent, a bike, and a laptop can come here and work on his or her pet project with a minimum of noise and distraction along the shore of Parvin Lake or in the Thundergust Lake cabins. And somehow you'll sense that time goes just a little bit slower here in the pinelands fringe than it does everywhere else.

Parvin has an unsettling but fascinating history. Significant evidence exists for the use of this area by the Delaware tribe. Though no prehistoric sites have been identified, several arrowheads were discovered in the lakebed prior to dam construction after a flood in 1940. It's believed that a hunting camp was located somewhere along the watershed, and many prehistoric sites have been identified in other areas bearing the same Evesboro and Manahawkin Muck soils.

The original parcel was deeded to one John Estaugh in 1742, later to be purchased by the sawyer who originally impounded Parvin Lake to power his mill. The lands provided timber and gravel until 1929, when the state purchased the lake and surrounding woods.

Two successive Civilian Conservation Corps (CCC) encampments improved the park for public use, establishing trails, a larger beach area, Thundergust Lake (which resulted from the damming of a swamp), and the bridge to Flag Island. Closed in 1942, the barracks were used by migrant workers and, later, German prisoners of war who had been part of Rommel's infamous Afrika Korps. Following the war, the CCC camp was used to house displaced Japanese Americans—those previously moved to internment camps—who worked in the local farms and food production industry. Yet another group of displaced people were Kalmyck refugees, who had fled the Volga Basin area of the USSR under Stalin. About 300,000 of these people perished as they were deported to Siberia for harboring anti-Communist sentiment. Some escaped and made their way to Parvin.

Parvin State Park is 6 miles west of the mini-metropolis of Vineland (a curious sort of South Jersey Sunset Strip) on County Route 540 (Almond Road), and 7 miles northwest of Bridgeton. It can be reached easily off NJ 55 from interchange 35, or by traveling east on CR 540 from NJ 77.

When you get to the park, in addition to getting the free park map, ask for a copy of the excellent "Hiking and Walking Trails" map, which was created by the Parvin State Park Appreciation Committee (now, how many parks have one of those?) and is available for $1. This large (24- by 29-inch) map identifies all the trails accurately, which the handout map doesn't do. For accurate navigation beyond the areas covered in this book's text and map, the larger map is essential. I haven't described trails in the natural area (everything west of the Knoll Trail), because these trails may be off limits to mountain bikers in the future.

Begin from the main parking area, across CR 540, opposite the park office and the bathhouse. As you face the bathhouse, turn left onto the Parvin Lake Trail (green markers).

0.00 *Follow the Parvin Lake Trail, keeping the lake to your right.*

0.25 *Cross a bridge onto Flag Island.*

0.30 *Cross another bridge, and walk down the steps on the other side of the island.*

0.42 *Cross a dam with a view of Parvin Lake.*

0.49 *Go past Fisherman's Landing boat launch.*

0.60 *Cross a bridge. A small pond connected to the lake is on your left.*

0.65 *With a cabin on your left, cross Forest Road and go through a gate. The nature center will be on your right. You'll see a small parking area to your left, with room for three or four cars. Go left here, following close to the shore of Thundergust Lake, and find the trail, a narrow singletrack. Follow around the northeast end of Thundergust Lake.*

1.00 *Arrive at a picnic and play area on your left.*

1.36 *Cross a small wooden bridge over the feeder creek at the south end of the lake. Immediately across this bridge is a T. Go straight. (To the right, the trail goes through the cabin camping area, which you should avoid.)*

1.44 *At the four-way intersection of the Black Oak and Long Trails, turn left onto the Black Oak Trail.*

From this intersection you can see Cabin Road ahead and to your right. Now you're entering a more remote area of the forest over a doubletrack sand and moss trail.

2.45 *Reach a T. (Technically, this is a four-way intersection, but the left dead-ends at Morton Avenue, and straight ahead goes to the natural area.) Turn right and go straight through a large gravel pit (actually it's more like sand).*

2.52 *As you enter the woods again at the north end of the gravel pit, avoid the trail to your right and keep going straight.*

2.60 *At a four-way intersection where a smaller singletrack crosses the dirt road you're on, turn right onto the singletrack.*

This is the Long Trail, which is keyed as red on the map but won't necessarily be marked.

> Continue on the trail, watching carefully to your left for the Flat Trail.

2.68 Turn left onto the Flat Trail, which has no color designation yet; it's currently identified with yellow paint blazes.

2.72 Cross Forest Road and continue on the other side. Go across a pair of small plank bridges.

2.98 Recross Forest Road. As the trail reenters the woods on the other side of the road, a sign says HIKERS ONLY, but this trail is now legal to mountain bikes.

3.02 When you intersect with the Parvin Lake Trail (green), go left.

3.22 Come across a plank bridge and follow green markers to the right on broken pavement.

3.32 Cross an oddly constructed (to keep motorized vehicles out) wooden bridge over Muddy Run Stream. Watch carefully for the next right turn.

3.40 At an intersection, take a right turn on the Parvin Lake Trail, which is well marked in green blazes.

> This area is heavily grown over with cedar, holly, and oak trees.

3.94 Bear left at a Y, following green markers. Soon you'll see a fence to your right, and the road (CR 540) to your left. You'll pass an extensive picnic area.

4.37 Arrive back at the park office and bathhouse.

You can pick up additional mileage by touring back to the south side of Parvin Lake, following the Parvin Lake Trail past Island and Jaggers Points, and riding the Forest Road Loop, returning on the Long Trail to Cabin Road or the Thundergust Lake Trail. Trail connections are confusing in the Lost Trail area, and exploring on your own is the best way to see this part of the park. This is also in the area where the most legal singletrack exists (roughly east of the gravel pit between Forest Road and the Black Oak Trail). Marking and designation of trails in this area is included in the unit management plans for Parvin State Park and may be in place by the time you visit. Be sure to inquire at the office about any trail changes or restrictions.

Information

Parvin State Park
RD 1, Box 374, Elmer, NJ 08318
609-358-8616

Bicycle Repair Services

Tommy's Bike Shop
Norma, NJ
609-692-9146

Beacon Cycling and Fitness
Vineland, NJ
609-696-2666

Resources

Advocacy Groups

Pedestrian/Bicycle Advocate
New Jersey Department of Transportation
1035 Parkside Avenue
CN 617
Trenton, NJ 08625
Write for New Jersey Bicycling Information.

New Jersey Air Quality Hotline
1-800-782-0160

Rails to Trails Conservancy
1400 16th Street NW, Suite 300
Washington, DC 20036

New Jersey Rail Trails
PO Box 23
Pluckemin, NJ 07978

D&H Canal Heritage Corridor Alliance
c/o The D&H Canal Museum
PO Box 23
High Falls, NY 12440
Write for Handbook for Action. A Guide to Building Partnerships for: Recreation,
Education, Preservation, Economic Development.

IMBA (International Mountain Biking Association)
5541 Central Avenue #201
Boulder, CO 80302
303-545-9011

JORBA (Jersey Off-Road Bicycle Association)
c/o Marty's Reliable Cycle
173 Speedwell Avenue
Morristown, NJ 07060
973-538-7773

NJCCC (New Jersey Cycling Conservation Club)
c/o Wally Tunison, The Bicycle Hub
455 Route 520
Marlboro, NJ 07746
732-972-8822

NORBA (National Off-Road Bicycle Association)
One Olympic Plaza
Colorado Springs, CO 80909

Adventure Cycling Association
150 East Pine Street
PO Box 8308
Missoula, MT 59807-8308
Expeditions, maps, technical/nutritional advice, advocacy.

New York Bicycling Coalition
PO Box 7335
Albany, NY 12224

Bike-Up America
Box 116
826 Proctor Avenue
Ogdensburg, NY 13669

Biking Is Kind to the Environment (B.I.K.E.)
Box 667
Chatham, NJ 07928

Pedals for Progress
86 East Main Street
High Bridge, NJ 08829
This organization reconditions bikes to send to South America. Newsletter.

League of American Wheelmen
The National Organization of Bicyclists
190 West Ostend Street, Suite 120
Baltimore, MD 21230-3731

Bicycle Federation of America
1506 21 Street NW, Suite 200
Washington, DC 20036-1008
Various pamphlets are available.

New York–New Jersey Trail Conference (NYNJTC)
GPO Box 2250
New York, NY 10116
(212) 685-9699
www.nynjtc.org/

Publications

Cycling Times
PO Box 1311
Fair Lawn, NJ 07410

Bike to Work Resource Guide
Craig Wolf
Chicago DOT, Room 406
121 North LaSalle Street
Chicago, IL 60602

The Complete Mountain Biker
Dennis Coello, 1989
Lyons & Burford, Publishers
31 West 21 Street
New York, NY 10010

Sloane's Complete Book of All-Terrain Bicycles
Eugene A. Sloane, 1991
Simon & Schuster
1230 Avenue of the Americas
New York, NY 10020

Mountain Biking: The Complete Guide
Sports Illustrated Winner's Circle Books
Time-Life Building
1271 Avenue of the Americas
New York, NY 10020

Women's Groups and Publications

Women's Mountain Bike and Tea Society (WOMBATS)
PO Box 757
Fairfax, CA 94978
24-hour hotline 415-459-0980
FAX 415-459-0832
Advocacy, workshops, newsletters, national chapters, events.

Mountain Biking for Women
Robin Stuart and Cathy Jensen, 1994
Acorn Publishing
1063 South Talmadge
Waverly, NY 14892-9514

A Woman's Guide to Cycling
Susan Weaver, 1991
Ten Speed Press
PO Box 7123
Berkeley, CA 94707

Cycling for Women
Editors of *Bicycling Magazine,* 1989
Rodale Press
33 East Minor Street
Emmaus, PA 18098

Let Backcountry Guides Take You There

More Biking Guides

In New England and the Northeast
25 Bicycle Tours in Maine, Third Edition
25 Mountain Bike Tours in Massachusetts
25 Bicycle Tours on Cape Cod and the Islands
25 Mountain Bike Tours in Vermont
25 Bicycle Tours in Vermont, Third Edition
25 Mountain Bike Tours in the Hudson Valley
25 Bicycle Tours in the Hudson Valley, Second Edition
25 Bicycle Tours in the Adirondacks
25 Mountain Bike Tours in the Adirondacks

In the Mid-Atlantic States
25 Bicycle Tours in Maryland
25 Bicycle Tours on Delmarva, Second Edition (now with 28 tours)
25 Bicycle Tours in Eastern Pennsylvania
30 Bicycle Tours in New Jersey
25 Bicycle Tours in and around Washington, D.C., Second Edition

Farther South, Farther West
25 Bicycle Tours in Ohio's Western Reserve
25 Bicycle Tours in Southern Indiana
30 Bicycle Tours in Wisconsin
25 Bicycle Tours in Coastal Georgia and the Carolina Low Country
25 Bicycle Tours in the Texas Hill Country and West Texas

We offer many more books on hiking, fly fishing, travel, nature, and other subjects. Our books are available at bookstores and outdoor stores everywhere. For more information or a free catalog, please call 1-800-245-4151 or write to us at The Countryman Press, PO Box 748, Woodstock, Vermont 05091. You can find us on the Web at www.countrymanpress.com.